PLAYING "all iN"

THE aspire... TO SERIES IS A COLLECTION OF BOOKS THAT PROVIDES LEADERS WITH REAL TOOLS AND PROVEN APPROACHES TO ALIGN THEIR TEAMS, CHALLENGE THE STATUS QUO, AND DELIVER OUTSTANDING RESULTS.

Also in the aspire... to series:

To contact Renie Cavallari, email renie@aspiremarketing.com
Visit www.aspiremarketing.com

RCI Publishing
PRINT: 978-1-5323-2897-8
E-VERSION: 978-1-5323-2898-5

Printed in the U.S.A.

aspire...
to shine

FOR THE THOUSANDS OF SHINERS WHO HELPED ME EXPLORE HOW WE AWAKEN OUR POTENTIAL. IN DOING SO, WE NOT ONLY MAKE A DIFFERENCE IN OUR OWN LIVES, WE MAKE OUR OWN MARK ON THE WORLD!
KEEP SHINING YOUR LIGHT...

DEDICATION

ER 93

THIS BOOK IS DEDICATED TO MY GRANDMOTHER,
MARTHA ADAMS. SHE WAS A SHINER.

28 June 1999

DEAREST GRAMS,

IT IS THOSE WHO SHINE THE LIGHT FOR OTHERS THAT QUIETLY LEAD THE WAY. IN MY LIFE YOU HAVE ALWAYS SHINED THE LIGHT TO HELP ME FIND MY OWN WAY. YOU HAVE BEEN AND SHALL ALWAYS BE MY HERO. THANK YOU.

I LOVE YOU,
Renie
XXOO

BE THE LiGHT

I was motivated to write this book by the many leaders I have had the privilege to work beside over the last 25+ years. Leaders who shined and leaders who seemed to be more committed to dimming the light. I never understood what the "light dimmer leaders" stood to gain.

For me, helping teams shine has been a gift in my life. I have, and continue to work on, a team of Shiners who are truly outstanding performers and humans. There is something that turns on from the inside as you watch others turn on from the outside.

"What the world needs now," as the song begins, "is love, sweet love."

Love is part of our ability to shine. Our love for our work. Our love for our teammates. Our love for others. Our pride in our contributions. Our commitment to care deeply about those we work beside and the customers we serve. It used to be that people believed there was no room for love in leadership. Today, we know it is those who lead from the heart that build sustainable and productive organizations where people love to come to work. Love does conquer many things…

I hope through reading this book you find some tips that help you be the leader you were intended to be. Leaders shine the light so that others can see what might not be as obvious. They light the way, decreasing fear so their people will take the calculated risks they need to have the life they want.

Leadership is a behavior, not a position. It does not matter what your job is or where you are on the proverbial organizational chart, you were meant to lead! We all lead though our influence and our impact. We lead through our attitudes. We lead through how we treat one another. We lead through the power of engagement.

Thank you for joining me on this leadership journey. As we lead in our own lives, we awaken our own potential. You were not born to play small and how you "self-lead" reflects how you shine.

When you shine the light, it always reflects back on you.

All in,

Renie

IN THIS BOOK

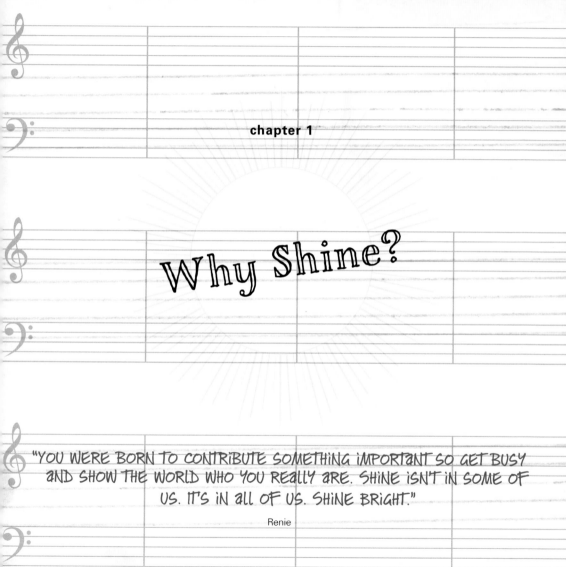

chapter 1

Why Shine?

"YOU WERE BORN TO CONTRIBUTE SOMETHING IMPORTANT SO GET BUSY AND SHOW THE WORLD WHO YOU REALLY ARE. SHINE ISN'T IN SOME OF US. IT'S IN ALL OF US. SHINE BRIGHT."

Renie

There are many reasons to shine and they vary for all of us. We tend to shine when we are doing things we love because the things we love bring us joy and we generally do them well. That is why we have to find what we love and value in our work — to align it with our own joy. When we shine, we have joy. Imagine a world full of joyful people!

The opposite is also true. When things in our life suck our joy, we don't shine.

In my years of research around "shining," I identified three interesting trends around why people shine and what influences them to shine:

1. OUR aBiLiTY TO aLiGN OUR PaSSiONS aND CONTRiBUTiONS WiTH OUR WORK aND LiFE

2. OUR CHOiCE TO BE aN aCTiVE LiFE PaRTiCiPaNT, "aN ENGaGER"

3. OUR KNOWLEDGE aROUND WHaT TRULY MOTiVaTES US

ALL THREE HELP US TURN ON OUR OWN MOTiVaTiONaL SWiTCH. WHEN YOUR SWiTCH iS iN THE "ON" POSiTiON, EVERYTHiNG iS POSSiBLE!

One thing is clear: we are all motivated differently and our motivations change with time and priorities. Some of us are motivated by the desire to make a difference in other people's lives while others are motivated by pride or a desire to outperform their competition. Regardless of what turns on your motivational switch, what is most important is knowing how to do it.

Shiner's Tip

UNDERSTANDING WHAT IGNITES YOUR PASSION IS USUALLY WHERE YOUR MOTIVATION LIES.

Some people hope for someone to motivate them. If you have children, you know that motivation comes from within! Trying to motivate another person is an impossible, never-ending task.

As a leader, you can only inspire people. You can't motivate them, so stop trying! The frustration you feel when you repeatedly attempt to motivate someone is because their motivational switch has only one operator… them!

In my research for this book, I interviewed and collected data from hundreds of highly motivated and not-so-motivated people. There is one overriding motivation for all of us:

OUR MOTIVATIONS REFLECT WHAT WE VALUE AND WHY WE CURRENTLY VALUE IT.

Your *"why"* allows you to explore your deeper reason for being on this planet — your true purpose. My purpose was clear early in my life. I found out how precious life was at an early age as I lost my brother when I was only four years old. It was a sudden, life-changing event and it threw my entire family into a deeply challenging time.

I came to realize that life was short — a hell of a lesson for a four-year-old. I learned you better live it while you can. This triggered my deep passion for life and provided a platform for me to be courageous in my decisions as I didn't focus on what I might lose in making a change. Instead, I focused on what I might gain.

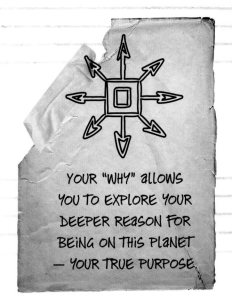

YOUR "WHY" allows YOU TO EXPLORE YOUR DEEPER REASON FOR BEING ON THIS PLANET — YOUR TRUE PURPOSE

My purpose still remains to *live my life with love and passion and positively touch lives.* When things get noisy in my life, reflecting on my higher purpose grounds me and gives me the clarity I need.

Clarity helps us make courageous choices and maintain internal alignment. It shines our internal light so we can get through the inevitable storms. Clarity is vital to helping us shine as when we are clear on what we want, we make decisions that serve us. Nothing dims our internal light faster than being out of alignment within ourselves.

I remember a recent time when I needed to make a different decision in my personal life and I kept putting it off. I became more and more irritable around the people who cared most about me. I didn't notice it but they sure did!

My choice to not make a decision was a decision and it was incongruent with what I wanted in my life. Even our bodies tell us when we are out of alignment with ourselves through that terrible feeling in the pit of our stomachs. We cannot shine when we are out of alignment within.

In order to understand what matters most, define what you value. Our actions reflect what we truly value so take a look at yours. For example:

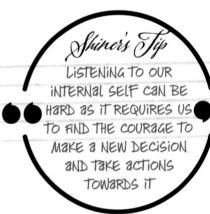

Shiner's Tip

LISTENING TO OUR INTERNAL SELF CAN BE HARD AS IT REQUIRES US TO FIND THE COURAGE TO MAKE A NEW DECISION AND TAKE ACTIONS TOWARDS IT

- If you value respect, you have to be respectful

- If you want to be recognized for the value you bring to your company, you must contribute beyond a mediocre level and truly perform

- If you want to make a difference, you have to help others see what is possible and shine the light their way

You do not shine alone. We are all dependent on others in some way. Maybe it is your boss or a co-worker. Maybe you are lucky enough to have a coach who can help you think and awaken your potential. If you hang with people who look for ways to improve their own lives, you too will be inspired to evolve.

> WE all NEED ENCOURAGEMENT.
> WHO ENCOURAGES YOU?

Years ago, I took my daughter to the water park.

She has always been a fearless adventurer and I will never forget our walking up what seemed like a thousand steps to the top of the biggest slide. She was full of excitement and anticipation while the "little people in my brain" (AKA self-talk) started talking trash. Loudly! *"What are we doing? Have I lost my mind? What if she gets hurt? What if I get hurt and she is alone? How high up is this slide? When is the last time the slide was checked for malfunctions? I wonder if their employees know CPR because I might just have a heart attack right now!"* You get the picture.

As we got to the top, my baby looked at me and said, "Don't worry, Mama! This is going to be so much fun!"

Shiner's Tip

" FORWARD MOMENTUM FUELS PROGRESS. "

Then she said, "Mama! Let me show you how to do it." She sat down on the pad and proceeded to tell me where and how to sit. She shared how to move with the curves of the slide. She told me to make sure there was water underneath my pad before I pushed off.

Shiner's Tip

" YOU WANT TO FIND THOSE PEOPLE WHO ENHANCE YOUR LIFE AND BRING ON YOUR SHINE. "

Then she showed me how. She went first and just before she hurled herself forward, she said, "Be sure to lean forward Mama. That makes it all the more fun!"

Then, with more enthusiasm than you can imagine, she was off like a bat out of hell. What a ride I had!

TAKE NOTE & CAST YOUR LIGHT

chapter 2

People Who Shine

"THERE IS NOTHING SO BRIGHT AS A PERSON WHO SHINES FROM WITHIN.
THEY ARE LIKE ELECTRICITY AND WE ALL WANT TO PLUG IN."

Renie

YOU KNOW THEM. THE PEOPLE WHO SHINE. THEY illuminate THE WORLD! THEY CHALLENGE THE STATUS QUO IN HOPES OF IMPROVING JUST ABOUT ANYTHING THEY CARE ABOUT AND HOPEFULLY THEY WORK FOR OR BESIDE YOU. I CALL THEM "THE SHINERS."

RC :)

Shiners are people who find what is right and build on it. This makes them interesting to be around and highly engaged. They inspire others to see what is possible and even imagine the impossible.

I love the Shiners. They aren't worried about popularity as they are disrupters. They have tenacity and don't mind a little mess to get things to a better place.

People who shine inspire others. They get people excited. Shiners push beyond the norms and limitations imposed by so many. They are demanding and even a pain in the ass as they want more; they do more; and yes, they innovate more. Shiners put themselves out there. They are daring.

People who shine are doers. They are not lazy and aren't interested in supporting mediocrity. They have tremendous pride in what they do and how they do it and this makes them highly competent. This competence allows them to contribute at an unusually high level which gets their heart racing. Shiners are proud people.

I was born in a suburb of Philly. A town where people are real and hard work is respected and expected. People love food, family, and hanging in their communities. They are neighborly and most people never leave. Philly is not as much about style and sophistication as it is about people and passion. You can see the passion and the honesty at any sporting event where a "Philly sports fan" will just as easily cheer on a home town player as boo him. It's a low-bullshit-threshold place. If you stink…you stink!

In Philly, it is your sense of engagement and passion that matters to most people. Like the community itself, we put a high value on your heart, soul and tenacity. Passion is in the blood of the city. It doesn't really matter where you live in Philly — the city or the suburbs — there is something about Philly that gives you permission to be who you are. People are bold.

Shiner's Tip

SHINERS GIVE TO THE COMMUNITIES THEY ARE COMMITTED TO — FROM FAMILY AND FRIENDSHIP TO WORK AND FELLOWSHIP

This is where I first learned what it meant to shine. "The Broad Street Bullies" (as we so lovingly referred to the Philadelphia Flyers hockey team when I was growing up) demonstrated "shine" through how they played. They had passion and tenacity and a commitment to never slow down. They pushed for every minute in every period of the game. They taught me what it meant to play "all in."

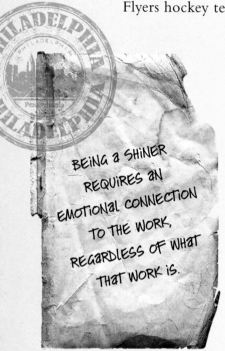

BEING a SHINER REQUIRES aN EMOTIONAL CONNECTION TO THE WORK, REGARDLESS OF WHAT THAT WORK IS.

Being a Shiner requires an emotional connection to the work, regardless of what that work is. This connection allows a Shiner to own their work and fanatically want to evolve it. No great artist lacks emotion. No great athlete plays without fierce energy and focus. Emotion evokes our passion and our passion fuels our world.

Shiner's Tip

SHINERS aRE "all iN" PLAYERS

"SHiNiNG iS a CHOiCE YOU MaKE. iT'S DELiBERaTE aND DEMaNDiNG."

Renie Cavallari

Shiners have three traits that provide consistent shine.
We call these the Shiner's Formula:

1. ENGaGEMENT:
SHiNERS aRE FaNaTiCaLLY ENGaGED. THEY WaNT TO aCTiVELY PaRTiCiPaTE aND
LEaRN aND aRE NOT aFRaiD TO TRY NEW THiNGS.
THEY SEaRCH FOR WaYS TO PRODUCTiVELY CONTRiBUTE.

2. SELF-LEaDERSHiP:
SHiNERS LEaD FROM WiTHiN.
THEY REaLiZE LEaDERSHiP iS a BEHaViOR, NOT a POSiTiON.

3. MOTiVaTiONaL SWiTCH:
SHiNERS KNOW HOW TO TURN ON THEiR MOTiVaTiONaL SWiTCH.
THEY UNDERSTaND THaT NO ONE ELSE CaN MOTiVaTE THEM...
THEY MUST DO THaT FOR THEMSELVES. THEY HaVE CHOSEN TO PLaY "aLL iN."

I first began to understand the power of shining when I developed an internship program for my employer 30 years ago. As is the case with internships, experience was not as important as an ability to be present. Internships were not easy to come by back then and we had hundreds of fantastic applicants.

It was a long process to get down to three finalists and it was Karen's exceptional engagement that landed her among them.

When I met with Karen, she shared she had come from a small town somewhere in the Midwest and her parents, though loving, didn't have high expectations of her. She did, however, expect a lot of herself. She was a farm girl. Not athletic, a little bit shy. The truth was she had not yet found her voice.

She was a good student with a full-time job as she needed to help pay her tuition. She had friends but found herself short on time because she had to work hard to maintain her 3.0 (B) average. She was certain that an internship would set her apart when the time came to find a "real job."

She did not have the best grades among our applicants nor did she come from the best college. She was not stylish nor overtly funny. And yet even now, years later, I can remember being struck by her positive energy and desire to do something extraordinary with her life, though at 21 she had no idea what. Karen stood out by her presence, her energy and determination. She got the internship.

I watched as Karen went from being a good intern into a great one. She interacted with everyone and worked hard to deliver any expectation put in front of her. (1. FANATICALLY ENGAGED!)

As an intern she clearly was not "leading" in the traditional sense but she knew that the way she connected and communicated would set her apart from others and it did. She intuitively understood she was a leader in her behavior, not in her position. (2. SELF-LEADERSHIP)

She wanted to learn and contribute. She loved being on a high performing team and she was "all in." (3. SHE KNEW WHAT MOTIVATED HER AND IT TURNED ON HER MOTIVATIONAL SWITCH)

Karen turned that internship into a permanent job. We had to have her! She was a Shiner. She went on to work for other companies and just ten years after that internship, she opened her own company. It was a huge success. Today she is an author, speaker, entrepreneur and business owner and she remains one hell of a human being! She is still the same small town girl at heart and her choice to shine laid the foundation to make her dreams come true. Long ago, she chose to be a Shiner.

Shiners don't need to be aspiring professionals, business owners or Vice Presidents. Shiners can be moms, students, gardeners, construction workers, or CEOs.

Shining has nothing to do with the job you have, the car you drive, or your income. Shiners shine through their participation in their life and this reflects in their work. Shiners engage, lead, and have their motivational switch in the full throttle position.

Shiner's Tip

SHINING IS NOT JUST A LEADERSHIP TRAIT. SHINING IS A HUMAN TRAIT. IT IS A CHOICE WE MAKE. EVERYONE CAN BE A SHINER!

TAKE NOTE & CAST YOUR LIGHT

chapter 3

Passion is Your Fuel

"WHAT I HAVE LEARNED ABOUT PEOPLE IS THAT THEY SHINE BEST WHEN
THEY HAVE AN OPPORTUNITY TO DISCOVER AND ENGAGE
THEIR PASSION."

Michael Stephens, Chief Enrichment Officer, Lansdowne Resort & Spa

Passion is the energy of your heart. The fuel of your life. It is the combustion of energy, emotion, and focus and it is at the core of people who shine.

Passion is an emotional state of mind. It drives you to engage and to perform at an outstanding level. Passion gives you the tenacity to persevere when others would quit or play small. Passion makes you consider more. Dare more. Be more. Live more. It allows you to make mistakes and move forward against difficult odds. Passion is unlimited energy and it positions you to achieve extraordinary results.

PASSION MAKES YOU
DARE MORE.
BE MORE.
LIVE MORE.

When you realize that mediocrity makes up 72% of the people in most normal organizations, you come to realize that when you awaken the passion in your people, you have a secret weapon in your toolbox.

You know that most people in a room will not play full out. Most will not be willing to put forth the extra effort nor push themselves into unfamiliar territory. They are unwilling to challenge things in search of better ways.

Everyone has passion but many of us are too afraid or lazy to tap into it. Sometimes passion is confused with emotion but emotion is only part of passion. Passion is the combustion of energy, emotion and focus. It comes together to fuel your soul.

Steve Jobs tapped into his passion and dared to change the way we worked, communicated and lived. Imagine not having a smart phone! No internet or music at our fingertips. No photos on hand unless we carry them in our wallets. Now we can have a 3-way call in a nanosecond or see another person on our phone while talking to them!

This visionary's passion allowed him to imagine things we did not know we would want, yet would come to depend upon. It was his passion that fueled the passion of so many of his fellow workers. It was his passion that so many of us admired and so many simultaneously feared. Steve said this about work:

"THE ONLY WAY TO DO GREAT WORK IS TO LOVE WHAT YOU DO. YOUR WORK IS GOING TO FILL A LARGE PART OF YOUR LIFE AND THE ONLY WAY TO BE TRULY SATISFIED IS TO DO WHAT YOU BELIEVE IS GREAT WORK. AND THE ONLY WAY TO DO GREAT WORK IS TO LOVE WHAT YOU DO. IF YOU HAVEN'T FOUND IT YET, KEEP LOOKING. DON'T SETTLE. "

Passion is not something you have to create. It is something that already exists within you and just needs to be unleashed. Here are a few ways to tap into your passion.

1. WORK FOR PEOPLE WHO HAVE PASSION FOR WHAT THEY ARE DOING. IF YOU WORK FOR A BOSS THAT LACKS PASSION, THEY WILL GENERALLY LIMIT YOURS.

2. AVOID PASSION KILLERS IN ALL WALKS OF YOUR LIFE. SOMETIMES YOU JUST HAVE TO FIRE PEOPLE. PERSONALLY AND PROFESSIONALLY.

3. UNDERSTAND WHAT INSPIRES YOU, NOT JUST WHAT MAY MAKE YOU SUCCESSFUL. WHEN YOUR WORK IS FULFILLING, YOUR PASSION NATURALLY COMES ALIVE AND YOUR LIFE IS NOT A STRUGGLE.

Michael Stephens, the Managing Director at Lansdowne Resort & Spa and a longtime leader in the hospitality industry, explores passion early on in the interview process. Here is what he believes:

"Passion is an essential part of getting to know someone's true spirit, understanding what makes them tick and what they are excited about in life. When I interview people, I first explore if they have passion in their life. I simply ask, 'What is it that you love and enjoy doing?' This single question allows us to understand if they are passionate. We only hire people with passion."

Passion drives us from a place deep inside. It is something that people connect with and if they agree with your views or feel comfortable with the energy that comes as a byproduct of your passion, they will embrace it... even delight in it!

I can personally attest that not everyone loves passionate people. I spent much of my early career being told to "tone it down" and play a bit smaller as my energy and passion were *too much*. When people aren't passionate about their lives, or when they fear your passion may cause change or adjustment for them, they tend to work extra hard to limit you.

Shiners shy away from people who lack passion.

I was blessed my father was an extremely passionate man. He used to always tell me that my passion for life was my gift. He gave me the quiet confidence I needed so I could know when to respect my audience and tone it down appropriately yet maintain my

passionate perspective around life and the things I believe in. He taught me how to champion the cause that was most important to me. My father instilled in me that passion was what would fuel me. He would say, "Baby, don't ever let anyone take away your passion or suggest you play small."

I have always felt sorry for those who have not yet tapped into their passion. Holding back your passion is not natural and is a learned behavior that doesn't serve you or the world. Think of how a child plays a game: they laugh, scream, and make new rules constantly. Children run in and out of the ocean, chasing waves with passion. They jump in and splash, scream, and carry on. It is the adults that say, "calm down" or, "don't splash." When we do this, we are creating a perspective or belief that to play full out is to play wrong!

IT IS PASSIONATE PEOPLE WHO CHANGE THE WORLD! CHOOSE TO BE ONE OF THEM!

We also teach our children that the way to play with others is to play quietly, play by the rules, and make 'nice-nice.' But what if they are filled with ideas? What if they are lucky enough to see the world in a full spectrum kaleidoscope of color instead of the three primary colors someone once dictated? To limit our children, and the child within us all, is to cap their passion and possibly their potential.

As parents, adults, friends, sisters, managers, and leaders, we must applaud passion in ourselves and those around us. We must create a never-ending state of imagination and unleash our passion for life! The passionate people on your team are those who will help you innovate, be a market-share leader, and challenge the status quo. It is passionate people who change the world! Choose to be one of them!

> ## Shiner's Tip
>
> TO LIVE YOUR LIFE WITH PASSION IS TO HONOR YOURSELF AND AWAKEN YOUR POTENTIAL. SHINERS DON'T FEAR THEIR PASSION. THEY EMBRACE IT AND WEAR IT WITH PRIDE!

1. Stop and think about what you love. What are the things that bring you joy? What makes you engage and how can you have more of it in your life? Don't think about the limitations. Look for the small opportunities and you will be surprised how they begin to present themselves.

2. Only work for passionate people. I know, how dare I say that! Am I suggesting you quit and find a passionate boss? Absolutely! Passionate people shine and if you want to be a Shiner, you have to be free to embrace and celebrate your passion. Then you can find ways to make your work align with your passion and this brings you joy... the ultimate goal of a happy life.

3. Use your passion as a motivator. Understand why you are here and how your work supports the bigger purpose: why the organization you work for exists. This will allow you to lead yourself and others more effectively. Why is at the heart of what people care about. Know your WHY!

4. Your passion aligns with what you value. Together, they are the light that shines off in the distance and calls to you, helping you when you lose your way.

5. Make work fun! You don't need a fun committee (though I was once asked to lead one). Take the lead and just try having some fun! Laugh often and don't be afraid to laugh loudly. Others will begin to wonder what they are missing.

6. Try new things. Dare to step out of your comfort zone and experience the many facets of life. Stop doing the same boring things and expecting to feel different!

7. Never let others tell you that your energy needs to be contained or is a problem for you. Use it to your advantage. This is not to say that obnoxious behavior is acceptable, just that energy is life.

8. Know that passion is your sword. Regardless of your life events, you can live with passion in a moment's notice. Just decide to live with passion. Do it now!

> " *Shiner's Tip*
>
> WHEN YOU SHINE, YOU ARE PASSIONATELY ENGAGED. LIFE IS TOO SHORT FOR ANYTHING LESS. WHY RIP YOURSELF OFF? YOU DESERVE TO LIVE BIG. TURN ON YOUR PASSION... NOW! "

ENERGY RADIATES POTENTIAL

Life is energy! When you are dead, you are technically out of energy. How you experience life reflects the type of energy you generate.

When we are tired and sick, we have low energy, causing us to move and think slowly. When we are well rested and in great health, the opposite is true.

All effort requires energy. Our energy is nourished by our motivation, engagement and state of mind.

Some people are energy suckers. They latch onto your energy and suck it dry. It is important to give our energy, and it is also important to set boundaries and protect it from abuse.

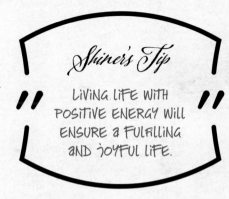

Shiner's Tip

LIVING LIFE WITH POSITIVE ENERGY WILL ENSURE a FULFILLING aND JOYFUL LIFE.

I am lucky. I was born with an extraordinary amount of energy! My father told me early on that my abundant energy was a gift and it would never let me down. Thank goodness he instilled the belief that if you are blessed with an endless reserve of positive energy, you must not be afraid to use it. High energy turns into passion so energy is a good thing!

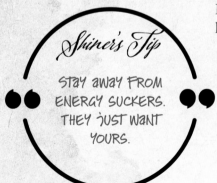

Shiner's Tip

STAY AWAY FROM ENERGY SUCKERS. THEY JUST WANT YOURS.

Life is an energy current exchange and the kind of energy you put in is the kind you get out. Energy varies in intensity and either serves or depletes you. It also impacts others. The same is true of others' energy as it can affect you. Here, I have identified 20 kinds of energy and their impact:

THE COLORS OF ENERGY

1. INSPIRED energy is stimulated, brilliantly creative, surpassing excellence
2. SENSUAL energy is sexual with a dose of intensity
3. OVERWHELMED energy is scattered and disorganized
4. INTENSE energy is demanding and focused. It can be helpful when you are pushing through fear or physical challenges
5. FOCUSED energy is tenacious and powerful
6. ELECTRIC energy is lively, happy and engaging
7. DIZZY energy tends to be more silly and giddy
8. SOFT energy is gentle and kind
9. AGILE energy is helpful and flexible
10. RELAXED energy is calm, meditative and easy
11. ANXIOUS energy is hurried, over-exerted energy delivered under pressure
12. OBSESSIVE energy is controlling and dysfunctional
13. AGGRAVATED energy is annoyed, angered, or ticked off
14. MEAN SPIRITED energy is powered by jealousy, resentment and revenge
15. COMMANDING energy is forceful and dictating
16. DARK energy is depression and high anxiety
17. NEGATIVE energy is fear-based and energy-sucking
18. INDIFFERENT energy is disengaged and checked out
19. LETHARGIC energy is lacking enthusiasm, tired, uninspired
20. DIM energy is indistinct, confused, unclear

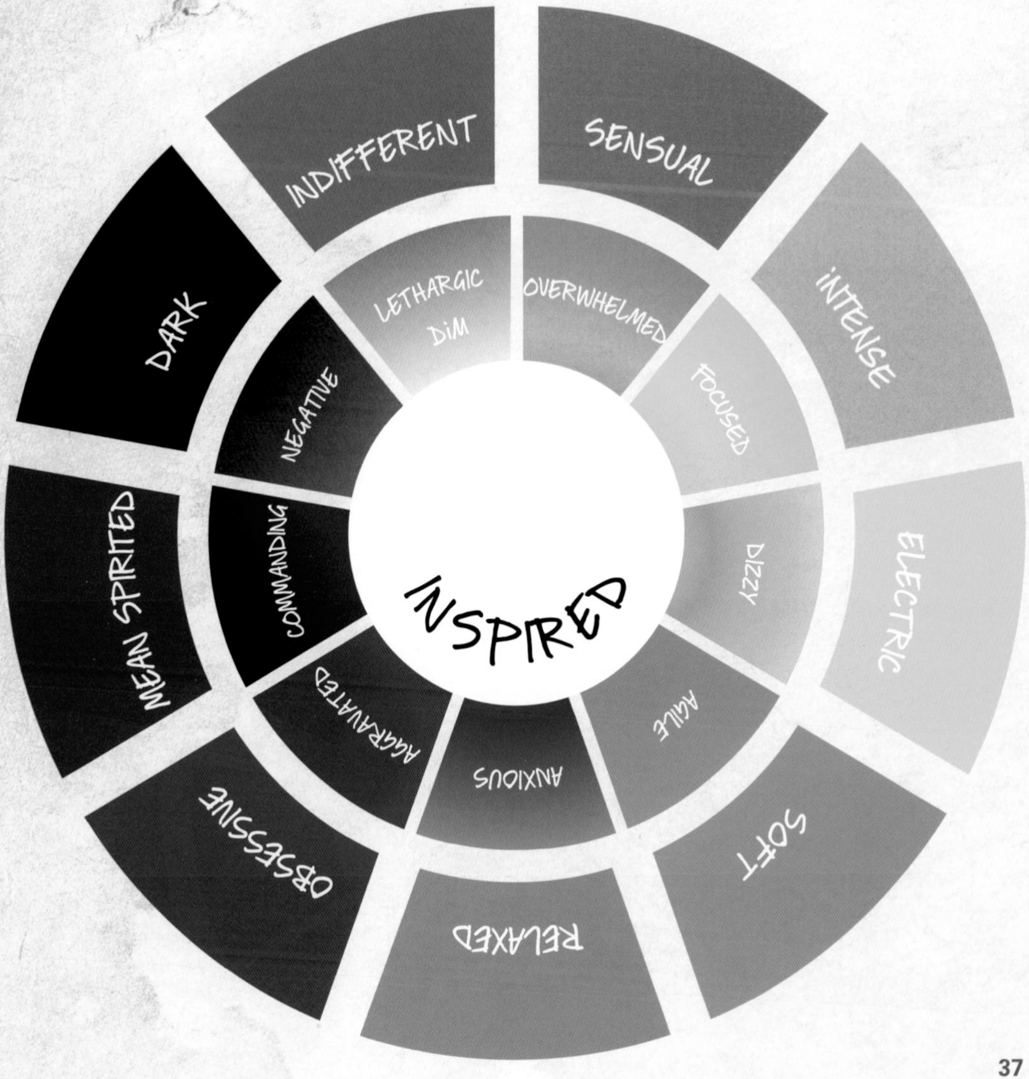

SENSUAL

INDIFFERENT

DARK

MEAN SPIRITED

OBSESSIVE

RELAXED

SOFT

ELECTRIC

INTENSE

LETHARGIC

DIM

OVERWHELMED

FOCUSED

DIZZY

AGILE

ANXIOUS

AGGRAVATED

COMMANDING

NEGATIVE

INSPIRED

TAKE NOTE & CAST YOUR LIGHT

chapter 4

Environmental Hazards

"SUCCESS BREEDS SUCCESS. ENTHUSIASM BREEDS ENTHUSIASM. AS LEADERS, THE MORE WE CREATE POSITIVE ENVIRONMENTS, THE MORE OPPORTUNITIES WE CREATE AND THIS BREEDS MORE SUCCESS. POSITIVITY, LIKE ENTHUSIASM, IS CONTAGIOUS."

Debbie Johnson, President and CEO, Arizona Lodging & Tourism Association

As the saying goes, "who you hang with is who you become." In other words, the people who surround you reflect the quality of your life. When you choose to hang with people who are supportive, you feel more internal fortitude to strive and thrive. Likewise, if you hang with people who are negative, pointing out what is wrong and only seeing the endless obstacles ahead, your mindset limits you and you too become a naysayer or "puker."

A WORD ABOUT THE NAYSAYERS... THE PUKERS

Pukers are light dimmers. They douse your light and limit your ability to shine. They are petty, even nasty, and especially like talking poorly about other people. Pukers see the problems in everything verses striving to help contribute to solutions and progress. Pukers undermine your work and your life.

YOU KNOW THEM. THE PUKERS OF THE WORLD. THEY "THROW UP" ALL OVER JUST ABOUT EVERYTHING.

I USE THE WORD PUKER TO HELP YOU VISUALIZE HOW THESE PEOPLE IMPACT YOUR WORLD.

WORSE YET, PUKERS DON'T LIKE TO PUKE ALONE. They look for those who are weak —those with less power or position — and they embrace them with their blame-and-shame perspectives. They kill positivity and productivity and like a cancer, they need to be cut from your team, whether it is your business team or your home team.

Am I suggesting you leave your job if your boss is a puker? Maybe! If your co-workers are pukers, don't let their negativity stick as only you can control how you feel and think.

As a speaker, when I discuss 'The Pukers of the Universe,' there is always someone in the audience who asks, "What if my husband (or mother or sister) is a puker? I can't just cut them out!" Maybe not. You can control how they will affect you, though. Set boundaries so their negativity does not become a part of you. Ask them to explore their negativity and share how sad you are that it prohibits their own potential. Tell them it sucks the life out of you. Yes, it is a tough conversation to have and it is your life!

> ## Shiner's Tip
> " THE QUALITY OF YOUR RELATIONSHIPS (BUSINESS AND PERSONAL) ARE NOT DEFINED BY THE HAPPY MOMENTS. THEY ARE DEFINED BY HOW YOU GET THROUGH THE CHALLENGES. "

PUKERS at WORK

Just because you work beside someone does not mean they have control over how you see the world and, more importantly, how you choose to participate in it. Ensuring each person on your team actively creates an energizing work environment is critical to your team's success.

Let's look at start-ups. They all start with visionary leaders. The crazy ones who see things others haven't yet imagined. Their passion for their work is contagious and many times people work for them for free... just to be a part! Over time, the lucky ones succeed and grow. The organizations that stay true to their vision and values survive growth. Those that lose their heart and soul struggle (and many die off) as the fight becomes about power, money and ego.

> JUST BECAUSE YOU WORK BESIDE SOMEONE DOES NOT MEAN THEY HAVE CONTROL OVER HOW YOU SEE THE WORLD AND, MORE IMPORTANTLY, HOW YOU CHOOSE TO PARTICIPATE IN IT.

The successful start-ups have an innovative concept but not all concepts make it past POC (proof of concept). What they have that drives them forward are fanatical people who create an environment that fills their tanks. When environments lose their positivity, their purpose and their intensity, they tend to lose their way. It's the environment that is the common thread to this reality. As leaders you have to create a healthy, productive, sustainable environment and then vehemently protect it.

I once worked with an organization whose HR Director — the person with a human talent development title and a role intended to celebrate the human spirit — was commanding and controlling, breaking rapport and destroying relationships. In one meeting I attended, they stole others' ideas outright and presented them as their own. Problem was, they had the boss's ear and as the staff was strong-armed, the top leader ignored the problem, denying its source. The culture became quietly toxic and the senior leadership team became highly dysfunctional. Even the top notch performers failed to perform. This team, which was once so inspired and highly engaged, fell apart. They went from a team who was "all in" to one that simply existed as a mediocre crowd.

It was like watching black ink dropped in a glass of water. The black droplet dissipates, quietly turning the entire glass gray.

We never want our team to deteriorate to that level of dysfunction, so how can we halt or reverse the unravelling of a team when we first recognize it? By having the courage to stop, ask, listen and explore the roots of the problem so it can be addressed.

RULE # 1 ON a TEAM is TO PROTECT THE ENVIRONMENT.

It is everyone's job to protect the environment. When there is toxicity, it affects everyone. It is true we are all human beings with fears and worries. Even positive people have toxic moments! We must stop it if (and when) we recognize it. As leaders, we must have the strength and courage to speak out when our community is going south. The higher up the food chain we are, the more responsible we have to be about protecting the environment.

In my role as a strategic coach, I see many toxic environments. They are always a significant cause of underperforming organizations. People are not inspired, aligned or engaged. Team members blame and shame one another vs. working to solve and resolve issues. Dysfunction and fear run rampant vs. connection and positive energy. Pettiness that frequently started innocently ramped up and became deadly.

> **Shiner's Tip**
>
> IT TAKES COURAGE TO CHALLENGE A TOXIC ENVIRONMENT. SHINERS ALWAYS FIND THE COURAGE.

Toxic environments are a reflection of leadership. These environments create what I call "human toxic waste." Like cancer cells in the body, if they are not carefully watched, they take over and destroy the potential of not just the team, but its members as well. The entire organization's health suffers.

Debbie Johnson, the President and CEO of Arizona Lodging and Tourism sheds light on a negative perspective like this:

"NEGATIVITY BREEDS NEGATIVITY. WE ALL HAVE BAD DAYS. THE CHALLENGE IS WHEN PEOPLE ONLY HAVE BAD DAYS."

Toxic environments are filled with pessimism and negativity. Nothing positive comes from negativity and though it is the leader's job to set an inspiring and engaging work place, it is everyone's job to contribute to making it better and ensuring its ongoing health.

At my company Aspire, a firm built around touching lives and developing the potential of people, we have only two fundamental rules:

1. BRING JOY TO OUR WORK PLACE EVERYDAY

2. ALWAYS BE PREPARED TO WORK YOUR ASS OFF ON BEHALF OF EACH OTHER AND OUR CLIENTS. OUR RELEVANCY IS ONLY DEFINED BY THEIRS.

People create the culture that defines our environment. That is why a "credo card" is worthless unless leaders lay the groundwork for bringing it to life. We are all a product of our environment and if leaders don't play "all in," you can bet their people won't! If leaders consistently find what is wrong and disempower their people, you will observe that even small mistakes can't be remedied without the leader actively involved.

Ineffective environments are breeding grounds for mediocrity. When people feel small, they act small so mediocrity becomes commonplace. Mediocrity lowers our expectations and makes us lazy. It kills any chance of shining. It's a light dimmer.

Shiner's Tip

YOUR ENVIRONMENT IS CRITICAL TO YOUR ABILITY TO PERFORM AND SHINE

HUMOR AND FUN HELP PEOPLE SHINE

Sometimes we need a little "recess" so we can re-engage and focus. Playful environments are usually more creative. Authoritarian environments may appear more productive but they lower energy and energy feeds the soul.

It is important to understand that successful environments balance positivity and fun with focus and discipline. It is the high positivity – high productivity environment that drives sustainable results.

I JUST CAN'T "ADULT" TODAY.

I'M AT RECESS.

DO NOT DISTURB.

Creating a high positivity – high productivity environment is everyone's job, not just the leaders'. When team members work together to create engaging and inspiring environments, people work with – and from - their heart. They aspire to more. They think together. Solve problems more effectively. Decrease costs and waste. They shine the light.

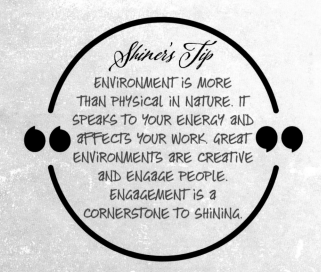

Shiner's Tip

ENVIRONMENT IS MORE THAN PHYSICAL IN NATURE. IT SPEAKS TO YOUR ENERGY AND AFFECTS YOUR WORK. GREAT ENVIRONMENTS ARE CREATIVE AND ENGAGE PEOPLE. ENGAGEMENT IS A CORNERSTONE TO SHINING.

TAKE NOTE & CAST YOUR LIGHT

chapter 5

What does it mean to Shine?

"WHEN PEOPLE ARE INCLUDED INTO THE CONVERSATION THEY FEEL
VALUED AND THIS TURNS ON THEIR MOTIVATIONAL SWITCH.
I LIKE TO ASK : 'I WANT TO KNOW IF YOU OWNED THE PLACE,
WHAT WOULD YOU DO DIFFERENTLY?'"

Rick Riess, Managing Director, Montage Resorts

For the majority of my career I have been a strategist by discipline. Simply put, my job is to figure out how to optimize people and assets to disrupt the status quo, identify where uncharted possibilities lie, and help others see a future they may not yet even imagine.

This work helped me understand that though strategy development was my initial responsibility, the real deliverable was to bring the strategy to life. It was a humbling experience to realize how difficult that actually was! My "awakening" took me 17 months, 14 days and 7 hours when my boss promoted me to lead the execution of my many "creative" strategies. Leading an operations team made things crystal clear. I had been seriously confused about what mattered most — strategy or culture — for years!

It is no secret that people are the foundation for all success or failure regardless of the strategy. As an operations leader, I quickly learned that for people to truly perform at an outstanding level, they had to strategically and emotionally align with the organization's strategies.

Alignment is the single greatest ingredient to achieving optimal productivity and this sets the stage for teams to shine. Teams that align, shine! And teams that shine outperform others.

It doesn't matter what the business is... THE MORE ALIGNMENT, THE MORE SYNERGY... and this creates MOMENTUM. Momentum leads to PROGRESS. Progress drives IMPROVED RESULTS.

In order to pursue a deep understanding of how to ensure strategic objectives come to life, I obsessively studied the differences between performers who were capable of sustaining truly outstanding performance and the others with great potential who were mediocre performers at best.

For more than 21 years, Aspire has analyzed performers in a variety of industries to identify the various characteristics, behaviors, skills, mindset and other factors that make some people shine while others barely get by. We didn't realize it in the beginning, but we have been on a passionate pursuit to fill the world with Shiners!

Through our research, we identified 4 levels of performance which I detailed in my previous book, *aspire...to lead*. Here are the highlights:

Shiner's Tip

IMAGINE EVERYONE IN YOUR ORGANIZATION ENGAGED, ALIGNED AND PERFORMING TO THEIR POTENTIAL. IMAGINE EVERYONE PLAYING "ALL IN!"

4 LEVELS OF PERFORMANCE

OUTSTANDING PERFORMER
SUPERSTAR SHINER

- THE BEST OF THE BEST
- FANATICALLY FOCUSED
- TAPPED INTO THEIR PASSION
- DISRUPTIVE AND DEMANDING
- INSPIRED ENERGY
- CONSISTENTLY DELIVERS BEYOND EXPECTATIONS

4%*

TOP NOTCH PERFORMER
SHINER

- STILL AN "A" PLAYER LIKE THE OUTSTANDING PERFORMER
- HIGHLY SKILLED AND FOCUSED
- LEARNER MENTALITY: HIGH DESIRE FOR MORE
- CONSISTENTLY DELIVERS TO EXPECTATIONS
- HIGHLY RESPONSIBLE AND ACCOUNTABLE

17%*

MEDIOCRE CROWD

UP-AND-COMING SHINER

NAYSAYERS / PUKERS

HOPEFULLY WORKING FOR YOUR COMPETITION SOON!

- IF THEY DON'T GET THE LEADERSHIP, INSPIRATION AND COACHING THEY NEED, THEY WILL BECOME A NAYSAYER

- AN ASPIRATIONAL SHINER IF COACHED OR A POTENTIAL NAYSAYER DEPENDING ON WHOM THEY HANG WITH

- NEED COACHING TO DEVELOP OR EXPAND SKILL SET - MAY BE NEW TO A JOB OR COMPLACENT FROM BEING IN SAME JOB TOO LONG

- HIGHLY INFLUENCED BY THEIR ENVIRONMENT, POSITIVE OR NEGATIVE

- ACCOUNTABILITY IS VITAL TO MOVE THEM TO THE NEXT LEVEL

- LIGHT DIMMERS

- ENERGY SUCKERS

- BLAME AND SHAME

- THEY PUKE ALL OVER EVERYTHING, FINDING WHAT'S WRONG AND STAYING FOCUSED ON THE PROBLEMS

- A CANCER INSIDE YOUR ORGANIZATION THAT NEEDS AN EXIT STRATEGY

72%*

7%*

*Percentages based on the average team

As we studied these performance levels, there was a burning question that had to be answered:

HOW DO YOU GET EVERYONE ON a TEAM TO PLaY aT THE OUTSTaNDiNG OR TOP NOTCH LEVELS?

HOW DO YOU MOVE THE MEDiOCRE CROWD UP THE PERFORMaNCE MODEL aS QUiCKLY aS POSSiBLE?

One thing became clear early in our analysis. Performance is always moving up (improving) or down (declining).

What is equally as compelling is that your performance is directly reflective of three key competencies. We call these the Aspire Competency Set®.
1. Mindset
2. Skill Set
3. Process Set

We consistently saw these competencies in the outstanding and top notch performers so we conclude these competencies are at the heart of moving mediocre performers up the performance model.

In addition, no matter the job, the "sets" were predictive indicators of a person's ability to perform. The great news is that "the performer" displays all three competencies. Therefore, as a coach and leader, you know how to help your people improve their performance specifically. Let's take a closer look.

"IF YOUR HEAD AND HEART AREN'T INTO WHAT YOU ARE DOING, NO AMOUNT OF TRAINING, COACHING OR SUPPORT WILL HELP YOU."

:) :

YOU DECIDE

JC Thompson, SVP, Aspire

Your mindset is how you see the world whether you are doing your job, cleaning your house, or playing golf. Your mindset is the perspective you hold. Simply put, your perspective serves you or limits you. It goes beyond being an optimist or pessimist.

YOUR MINDSET IS HOW YOU FEEL WHICH DEFINES HOW YOU THINK.
HOW YOU THINK DETERMINES HOW YOU ACT, RESPOND OR PERFORM.

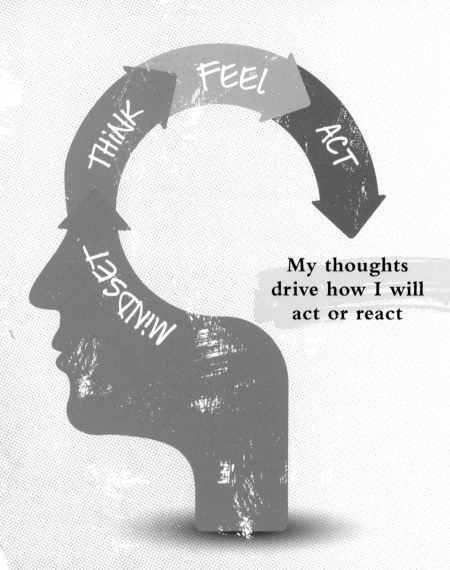

THINK

FEEL

ACT

MINDSET

My thoughts
drive how I will
act or react

SELF-TALK...THE LITTLE PEOPLE IN YOUR HEAD!

You may be aware that your brain is full of "little people." You may know them as your self-talk. They are your thoughts.

Thoughts are powerful beyond words. They set the tempo of our life and increase or deplete our energy. Positive and supportive thoughts make you feel a whole lot different than negative and limiting ones do. It is vital to understand that how you **FEEL** is a derivative of how you **THINK**. If you want to change anything, you must start with what you think. Your thoughts define your feelings and how you **FEEL** determines how you will **act**.

" *Shiner's Tip*

YOU FEEL
THE WAY YOU THINK "

EVERYONE KNOWS WHAT YOU ARE REALLY THINKING BY YOUR ACTIONS (YOUR BEHAVIORS THAT ARE A RESULT OF YOUR THOUGHTS AND FEELINGS), NOT BY YOUR WORDS.

John was just promoted to a regional role at his company. In his previous job, he won many awards and was recognized as an outstanding Food & Beverage Leader. John knew how to run a restaurant, was an excellent chef, understood how to make an operation profitable and was good at training his people to serve with "pleasure" as he often mentioned. John was excited about his promotion.

Six months into this new position, John's boss told him he was failing. His team was not performing and according to his boss, he was not well liked. His directions and decisions may have been right but that wasn't his job any longer... it was his onsite manager's job. His new job was to get others to know how to do their jobs. His responsibilities had changed, yet his mindset (thinking) had not.

As John started to explore what was going wrong, it became clear he had been operating from a misunderstanding about his role and responsibilities. He felt that because he knew all the answers, there was no need to engage others into conversation. He thought, "I can make things happen a lot faster if I just tell others what to do and how I want it done." You can imagine his behaviors with that kind of thinking! The result? His most talented people were leaving the company in droves.

John thought he had all the answers and his belief (your beliefs are absolute thoughts) was that he could get more done by telling people what to do vs. engaging them into the solutions and opportunities he wanted to leverage. He was your typical "control and command" manager which worked in a small operation. It did not play out well in a larger role.

John did not intend to offend his leaders and yet, he had. He wanted fast progress and his thoughts (do it my way) led his actions (or else) which in turn caused his talent to leave, or worse yet, stay and not play "all in."

For John to move from a fast and furious efficiency (I know the answer and I just need my people to execute) to a more effective approach (coach onsite leaders to find solutions themselves), he had to learn new leadership skills and most of all, he needed to learn to coach. This was the only way he could help others shine and become successful in his regional role.

Let's take a look at what it takes to truly develop a team and help them shine... Coaching.

COACHES COACH

Coaching is not about having the answer. It is a mindset of helping others find the answer! Coaching is different than managing as management is facilitating people, product and process. Managing is mapping and directing whereas coaching is engaging and optimizing the potential of people.

Coaching requires patience, time, preparation and commitment on behalf of the person you are coaching. Coaching is a gift we give and when we are being coached, it is a gift we must be open to receiving. Coaching requires a platform of rapport and trust so connection is required if you are to reach ideal success.

A coach is there to help people step outside of their comfort zone and grow. This is a huge request of another person as it means they have to let go of control. Progress occurs no other way. Everyone supports progress, yet some people want it to come without having to change or participate in it. Progress does not occur that way. A great coach stimulates engagement and a desire to come back for more.

Asking questions is a great tool to help you coach effectively as a leader. It is important to shift focus, engage thinking, and explore other ways of doing things. When we ask open-ended questions like those below, we open up the conversation and allow people the mental space to explore and learn.

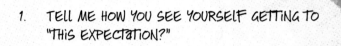

1. TELL ME HOW YOU SEE YOURSELF GETTING TO
    "THIS EXPECTATION?"

2. WHAT WILL YOU GAIN WHEN YOU MEET THIS EXPECTATION?
    WHY DO YOU WANT TO?

3. WHAT OBSTACLES DO YOU NEED REMOVED SO YOU CAN GET
    WHERE YOU NEED TO GO?

4. WHAT WILL YOU NEED TO DO DIFFERENTLY TO OVERCOME
    "THIS UPSET?"

5. HOW DO YOU WANT TO BE PERCEIVED AS A LEADER? HOW WOULD
    YOU HAVE TO CHANGE YOUR APPROACH TO GET THAT RECOGNITION?

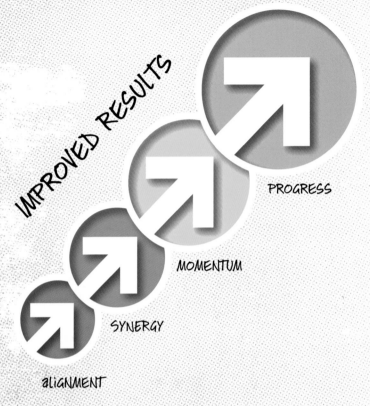

IMPROVED RESULTS

PROGRESS

MOMENTUM

SYNERGY

ALIGNMENT

As we stretch and awaken a person's potential, we need to understand their fear of failure. They may take two steps backwards without a guarantee of any steps forward. We must be willing to risk perfection for growth because perfection kills progress.

Encouragement moves people through the storms of making changes and progress comes no other way. Learning new skills or processes requires us to try new things. Good coaches encourage for encouragement lights the way.

COACHES ARE SHINER FINDERS. They are people potential junkies. They know that if a person has the right mindset, then learning new skills and processes will be easy. They inspire people to explore their internal motivation. They help tie a person's work to their own values and higher purpose. Smart coaches know there is no point in coaching someone who doesn't want to change.

Your success reflects your effort and commitment and though a great coach can help you get there, in the end it's up to you to live to your potential.

Shiner's Tip

"A GREAT COACH WILL HELP YOU SHINE. A GREAT LEARNER WILL CHOOSE TO LET THEIR LIGHT SHINE."

COACHES SHINE THE LIGHT

"COACHES UNDERSTAND THAT WHEN IT COMES TO COACHING, THE ANSWER IS IN THE CHAIR OVER THERE. IT'S NOT THE COACH'S JOB TO HAVE THE ANSWER. IT IS THEIR JOB TO HELP OTHERS FIND THE ANSWER."

RC :)

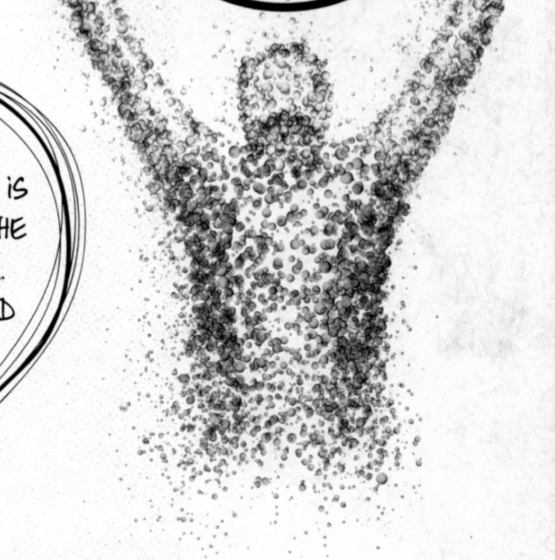

We were taught to write, speak and punctuate (along with other effective communication elements) all through our years in school and yet we never attended a class that had anything to do with acknowledging others! When you acknowledge what another person says, you ensure you understand their message. In addition, acknowledgment communicates to them that they are important enough to listen to and be heard.

When someone feels heard, they engage differently. They stop repeating themselves and also begin to listen. When we acknowledge what someone is saying, we demonstrate our compassion and respect for them. Most importantly, when people feel heard, they feel valued and included.

People often mistake acknowledgment for agreement. They are not the same thing! You don't have to agree in order to acknowledge. Acknowledgment is an act of compassion that brings people into the conversation you are trying to have. As a leader, you may often find yourself in a position to explore other people's mistakes or perspectives. Are you the kind of leader that makes them feel worse? If so, try to acknowledge their perspective when discussing what went wrong so you can engage them into correcting it.

IT'S THE MIND THAT MATTERS

When you understand that you feel the way you think, your thoughts define your beliefs, and those absolutes determine your behaviors and actions, you begin to see the critical need to ensure your thoughts are serving your best interest.

Shiner's Tip

" PEOPLE WHO are ACKNOWLEDGED are MORE LIKELY TO ENGAGE WITH YOU. FEELING VALUED MATTERS. "

Thoughts always drive feelings. Human beings are controlled by their minds (thoughts), not their hearts. Hallmark, the card company, may tell you differently and they don't know the truth about people! How you feel reflects how you are thinking. Your actions then align with those thoughts and feelings to support your direction.

> ## *Shiner's Tip*
> " THE LITTLE PEOPLE THAT LIVE IN YOUR BRAIN ARE POWERFUL. THEY SPEAK DIRECTLY TO WHAT YOU BELIEVE REGARDLESS OF HOW INSANE YOUR BELIEF MIGHT BE. BELIEFS ARE JUST ABSOLUTE THOUGHTS. THEY ARE THE RULES WITHIN US. "

EXPLORING YOUR MIND...

When things happen, the little people in your brain tell you how you will react or feel based on your thoughts and beliefs. These thoughts determine what actions you will take.

For example:
    Luke wants to take the family car out for a spin, against his parents' wishes. He feels he was grounded unfairly and his parents are out for the evening. He knows if he gets caught, there will be hell to pay and yet he takes the car anyway. Why?

Simple: Luke's thoughts tell him the odds are good he can get away with it. He justifies it by telling himself he shouldn't have been grounded in the first place! His behavior - taking the car - was predictable based on his thoughts and feelings about his punishment and his current situation.

The mind is both simple and complex. As humans, we observe and absorb information, add a bunch of noise, and then take action. Sometimes we can't figure out why we are doing something we shouldn't or worse yet, doing something we don't even want to do!

Understanding the power of our thoughts is vital to changing behavior which leads to improved performance (competency set). Leaders understand that getting people to change their behavior is a cornerstone to constant and never-ending improvement and future success. Changing people is impossible so don't bother wasting your time!

I once was working with a team that had been through an ugly takeover. Feelings were hurt and even years later, with the entire C team replaced, the residue remained. For the most part, the team members were mediocre as they resented the past mistreatment. Bitter may not look good on anyone and people wear it just the same!

The new leaders of the takeover team changed their approach. They aligned with a new higher purpose (vision) and established clear values that would lay the foundation for their company culture. Within nine months, that non-performing group became a high performance team.

These leaders didn't demand trust – they became trustworthy. They effectively communicated the new direction and their expectations. They implemented an accountable culture and coached that team to a much greater success than before the buyout. They inspired their people to change their mindset and everything changed: positivity, productivity and profitability, to name a few.

> PEOPLE DON'T CHANGE THEIR BEHAVIOR BECAUSE YOU TELL THEM TO. PEOPLE CHANGE BECAUSE THEY DECIDE TO. THEY CHANGE BECAUSE THEY FEEL EMOTIONALLY CONNECTED TO YOUR NEW DIRECTION.

Great leaders understand that the first step in improving a person's performance is to help shift their thinking so they are aligned and engaged. People don't change their behavior because you tell them to. People change because they decide to. They change because they feel emotionally connected to your new direction.

You can't control a person's choice to change anything. What can you control? Your expectations, accountability and coaching effectiveness. Apply that to any role in your life! As a parent, you can inspire your child. You can lead. You can coach. You don't have much control beyond implementing consequences and establishing accountability.

As a coach, understanding the brain is important to helping a person change their behavior, whether it be as simple as changing a process or as monumental as changing your business model.

LET'S TAKE a LOOK INSIDE THE 2 SIDES OF YOUR MIND.

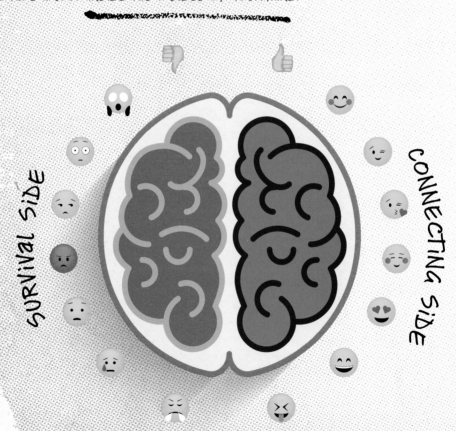

SURVIVAL SiDE

CONNECTING SiDE

- The survival side of the brain is where fear, worry, annoyance, anger, distress, problems, shortness of breath, irrationality and other levels of negativity live.

- The connecting side of our brain is where solutions, positivity, happiness, joy, objectivity, logic, solutions and other supportive feelings and actions live.

 HAPPENS

When it hits the fan, it is our thoughts and beliefs that determine which side of the brain we go to for help. That decision then defines how we will feel. How we feel (consciously or unconsciously) determines our behaviors. These actions define how we will experience life.

IT'S a MATTER OF PERSPECTIVE

Situation: Susan and Robin work in the same company for the same boss and both of them just got fired.

SUSAN'S PERSPECTIVE:
She feels relief and excitement
for what is next. She is
grateful for the experience
and the learning.

ROBIN'S PERSPECTIVE:
Robin is pissed. She feels
a sense of failure, fear and
anger. She is placing blame
on others.

SAME EXPERIENCE.
DIFFERENT MINDSETS = DIFFERENT PERSPECTIVES.
IMAGINE HOW EACH WILL ACT NEXT.

This example demonstrates why some people can see a situation and move into a solution mode while others experience the same situation and move directly into anger, worry and panic. It is a simple difference in their thinking, their mindset.

Shiner's Tip

DEMOTIVATING THOUGHTS SLOW UP PROGRESS AND LIMIT YOUR POTENTIAL. MOTIVATING THOUGHTS TURN ON YOUR MOTIVATIONAL SWITCH.

WHAT ARE YOU SAYING IN THERE?

Our mindset reflects the questions and self-talk our little people in our heads say to our inner-selves. If we state, "this will never work," the odds are pretty good it won't! We set up a negative thought when we ask a question like, "why did this happen to me?"

Likewise, if we have something happen and we find the strength to ask, "How can I leverage this experience to find what I was meant to do next?" or, "What about this will be a blessing for me in two years?" We may experience the same situation completely differently... and with much less nausea!

Changing our negative thoughts can be difficult. The best way to shift your mindset is by changing the questions you ask yourself. When you ask yourself a more empowered question, you can move from the survival side of your brain to the connecting side. Ultimately, the quality of your life reflects the questions you ask yourself and how your thoughts and beliefs support or disempower you.

When it comes to having the right mindset, your goal is to live in the connecting side of your brain as much as possible. Tips:

- FOCUS ON WHAT YOU FEEL GRATEFUL FOR WHEN YOU ARE STRESSED OR WORRIED

- FOCUS ON HOW THE SITUATION WILL HELP YOU IN THE FUTURE

- SHIFT YOUR THINKING BY ASKING YOURSELF A QUESTION LIKE, "HOW CAN I USE THIS SITUATION FOR THE BETTER?"

- REMEMBER: IF YOU HAVE THE WRONG MINDSET, THINGS LIKELY WILL NOT GO AS YOU HOPE.

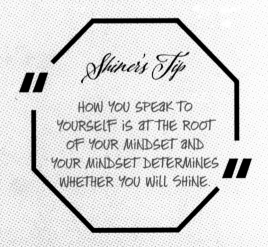

Shiner's Tip

"HOW YOU SPEAK TO YOURSELF IS AT THE ROOT OF YOUR MINDSET AND YOUR MINDSET DETERMINES WHETHER YOU WILL SHINE."

Life has hurdles. Excuses won't make them go away. The hurdles don't define our lives; it is how we choose to experience them! If your hurdles become your excuse(s) then your potential is always self-limited and you will never get the chance to truly shine.

As a Coach's Coach, I see it often. Someone will have outstanding job skills and process applications, yet they are no longer performing at an outstanding level. The job didn't change.   Their mindset did.

Their perspective towards the job; the boss; the expectations; or some aspect of their life made them adopt a mindset that limited their potential and desire to shine. Their little people were in there blaming, shaming and positioning them to focus on the wrong things.

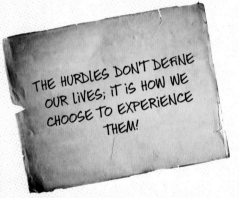

THE HURDLES DON'T DEFINE OUR LIVES; IT IS HOW WE CHOOSE TO EXPERIENCE THEM!

66

Shiner's Tip

YOU DECIDE YOUR PERSPECTIVE, THOUGHTS AND BELIEFS. THEY SERVE YOU OR THEY LIMIT YOU. THE CHOICE IS ALWAYS YOURS.

99

COMPETENCY 2: YOUR SKILL SET

No matter the job or activity, accomplishment requires skills and there are lots of ways to learn them. Sometimes you are lucky enough to work where someone is showing you the way. Good training is a gift as it allows us to learn and become competent with less challenge and embarrassment.

Other times, we learn on the job or worse yet, on our customers! In this case, it is up to us to find ways to learn the skills, perhaps by modeling others who are doing outstanding work or by putting in extra effort, to become competent as quickly as possible.

Skill sets vary. Most jobs require a multitude of skills. A sales person, for instance, needs sales skills as well as communication skills, strategic thinking skills, relationship building skills, and so on.

The Gardener in Me

A few years back I decided I was going to become a gardener. I wanted to have one of those beautiful courtyard gardens where everything is always blooming in full color. I didn't consider that beyond my endless travel schedule which would limit my ability to be around to take care of the plants – I have killed just about every plant I have ever purchased. When I see those plants at Trader Joe's, I am always drawn to buy another one. Why I keep doing this again and again remains a mystery to me!

None of that mattered. I had decided that I was going to have live art in my courtyard. I bought a few books and mostly looked at the pictures. I spent a small fortune on plants, tools, soil, fertilizer and pots of all sizes. I had a vision so my journey to become a *live art gardener* began!

I was enthusiastic at first (a strong mindset). I worked on it several days a week for months. Initially I didn't have appropriate skills so I gained them slowly through planting, killing, planting, improving... you get the picture. Over time I killed fewer plants but my learning curve was long.

Now you may be thinking, "what does gardening have to do with competency?" Everything! It drives home the point that if I had taken the time to read, watch videos or go to a class – perhaps even a 4-hour beginning gardener class - I would have saved time, money and all the disappointments that becoming a gardener actually required. Competency is a result of improving your skills. Without solid skills, your enthusiastic mindset will eventually dwindle. Mine did.

To shine, you have to be competent. Competency comes from our knowledge of what is expected, what to do (application of the skills) and how to do it (demonstration of the skills). We must apply our knowledge and be curious to learn more. The more we work at something, the more competent we become. This competency leads to confidence and confident people shine!

If you are lucky enough to have coaches, mentors and leaders who have built a platform for you to learn and grow, you should put this book down right now and send them a thank you note! Training and coaching from others is a gift, not a requirement.

Smart organizations have detailed plans on how to onboard and develop their people so they build and expand their skills and competencies. And in the end it is you who must be curious about how to do things differently and tenacious enough to go out there and sharpen your skills.

I now have a magnificent courtyard garden. After years of guilt (which lives in the survival side of your brain) for killing many plants and never investing the time to become the gardener I had hoped, I hired Barbara, my highly skilled and competent gardener, who has requested I stop touching her live art!

All I had to do was change my mindset. In order to get the result I wanted – a beautiful courtyard garden – I needed to think differently about how to get it. From the connecting side of my brain, I can see that Barbara shines when taking care of the plants and I shine from the joy and beauty they bring.

> *Shiner's Tip*
> LEARNERS always
> SHINE

COMPETENCY 3: YOUR PROCESS SET

Consistent accomplishment requires process. Sometimes we are conscious of the process and sometimes we are not. Conscious competency is always better!

Processes provide us with:

- A CONSISTENT approach for delivering results around a task or responsibility

- A SYSTEMATIC approach to continuous improvement

- LONG-TERM SUSTAINABILITY

- ALIGNMENT OF "HOW WE DO THINGS AROUND HERE"

- IMPROVED PRODUCTIVITY WITH FEWER ERRORS AND INCREASED EFFECTIVENESS

When we put the competency model into practice, we see results as ideal learning happens through an interactive, engaging and process-driven environment. Coaching is a skill that talented leaders draw on to build their team's skills and process improvement.

Coaching is awakening the potential of another person. Management is the facilitation of people, product and process. Talented managers provide processes for their people so they can become highly competent ...fast! The more quickly someone can do a job, the more productive they become. Productivity impacts profitability.

Let's take the process of cleaning a room: If you break it down into the 30 or 40 required tasks, it becomes easier for a housekeeper to learn what you expect and effectively complete the job. Without a process, each room becomes a new progression until a routine is established. The longer a person works on something, the more comfortable they are with the habit regardless of whether the habit is a smart one. We all know that habits are hard to break!

> ## Shiner's Tip
>
> " PROCESSES GIVE US CONSISTENCY, MAKE US CONSCIOUSLY COMPETENT AND ALLOW US TO CONSTANTLY IMPROVE "

Leaders want people with good habits who will effectively meet and exceed task expectations. Without processes, everyone does things their way which may not be the best or most efficient. In addition, you cannot step back and think strategically about how to improve a process if there isn't one to begin with. This limits your potential for constant and never-ending improvement — a direct correlation to profitability.

Years ago, I saw the power of process in action.
I was working with a truly outstanding sales person, Melinda. She could sell anything! She constantly moved her results forward and always exceeded expectations. Melinda was a star on the verge of shining. I remember when I sat her down and said I wanted to work with her on her sales process so she could take her talent to its next level. She was not pleased.

When I explored why she was so uncomfortable, she responded with a less-than-enthusiastic response, "Why mess with something that isn't broken?" As we talked through it, we agreed she would start to map out her approach to her day: how she thought, what she did, and why. She had great skills but I wanted her to be thinking about every step she took: the when and the why.

The first week was hard. She wasn't yet curious and it was a struggle. Then things started to unfold. Being conscious of her actions made her reflect on them. Melinda noticed that when she organized her target list on Friday, she worked differently on Monday.

She began asking herself why she would send certain things out to certain people and not to others. She began planning her days differently and tracking everything, which made her more competitive with herself.

This process opened up doors for Melinda. She learned to reflect on her sales processes and improve on them and she doubled her results over a 14-month period of time. When Melinda added thoughtful process to her strong skill set, she really started to shine. It was extraordinary.

For me, she gave me a model for how to create many outstanding sales people for years to come. A true gift when you are a Coach!

When we have clarity around a task's process, we can duplicate it and continue to improve on it. Defining her process gave Melinda the gift of becoming not just competent but *consciously* competent. Conscious competency builds confidence and confident people shine!

The unconsciously competent person is constantly wondering how they do what they do. They secretly fear they will not be able to replicate prior success or continuously deliver. Fear and worry impact mindset. It is scary to realize you are unconsciously competent as you become aware that you might not be able to improve or worse yet, consistently perform.

CONSCIOUS COMPETENCY BUILDS CONFIDENCE and CONFIDENT PEOPLE SHINE!

There is something special about a person with confidence. That sparkle in their eyes. The way they look at you, attract you to them, and engage you.

TaKE NOTE & CaST YOUR LiGHT

chapter 6

Leaders Shine the Light

"ORGANIZATIONS WITH HEART REFLECT THE LEADER'S ABILITY TO SHINE THE LIGHT."

JC Thompson, EVP, Aspire

In my book, *aspire…to lead,* I shared years of research and analysis around truly outstanding leaders and their approaches to leading high performance teams. It was through this research the 6 Pillars of Intentional Leadership™ originated.

As I toured the country talking about the Pillars over the past few years, I was inspired by many and the question they most often asked was:

"HOW DO I ALIGN MY PEOPLE AND GET THEM MOTIVATED SO THEY DO THEIR BEST WORK?"

This inspired me to interview hundreds of people over a 14-month period and to spend endless hours interviewing Shiners. One of the biggest findings was that over 90% of the Shiners I studied lived the 6 Pillars in their lives regardless of their position, responsibility, or time served. It didn't matter if they were a housekeeper, a sales person, a department head or a C, these same 6 Pillars were evident. In hindsight, it made perfect sense as all shiners lead from within.

Shiner's Tip

SHINE IS NOT IN SOME OF US. IT IS IN all OF US.

Leadership comes in many forms. There are those who are in positions of leadership and yet, leadership is a behavior, not a position. All of us have the opportunity to lead every day through the choices we make and the actions we take. This is self-leadership.

Self-leadership is leading from within and it awakens our true potential. It is an internal sense of knowing that the power behind your participation is how things come to fruition in your lives. Shiners are strong self-leaders.

When we see the leadership within ourselves, we understand we can make important things happen in large and small ways. This kind of leadership allows us to explore what else is possible in our lives and gives us the tenacity to create solutions to life's challenges.

Shiner's Tip

"" HOW YOU LEAD YOURSELF TELLS THE STORY OF YOUR LIFE. IT SAYS WHO YOU ARE. ""

Self-leadership is intentional and applies to all aspects of your life, both work and personal. When you lead from within, your confidence and poise shine through. Self-leadership helps you unlock your true potential, enhancing your relationships and life experiences.

1. CONNECTION

2. CLEAN COMMUNiCATiON

3. COMPASSION

4. HiGHER PURPOSE

5. PARTiCiPATiON – ENGAGEMENT

6. 100% RESPONSiBiLiTY = ACCOUNTaBiLiTY

Shiner's Tip

CONNECTiON BUiLDS RaPPORT aND TRUST aND SHiNERS BUiLD CONNECTiON.

Connection is the foundation of self-leadership and as with all of the Pillars, creating connection is an intentional act. Connection inspires us to work together for the good of our team. It is the rapport you build through getting to know someone on a human level. Connection is different than chemistry. Chemistry comes naturally, whereas connection is something you choose to build with another person. You have to work at connection, especially with those who may not think or act like you.

Connection builds rapport and rapport grows over time into trust. Where there is trust in any relationship you play differently together: you are less likely to second guess another's intention and you tend to be less defensive or critical when things get bumpy.

When it comes to communication, most of us are good talkers and lousy listeners. We spend most of our lives multi-tasking and are so crazy-busy, we simply can't focus or be present. Most upsets and confusion result from poor listening. Shiners listen more than they talk.

"IT'S NOT WHAT YOU SAID, IT'S HOW YOU SAID IT?"

Everyone's Mama

How you communicate dictates your effectiveness. In business relationships or with friends, family and loved ones, being direct is not always the best way to communicate. Clean communication is different than clear communication. Clean communication requires you to say what must be said in a way another person can have it verses just saying it outright or not saying it at all in an attempt to be nice. Poor communication creates drama and upsets. *No* communication can create stories in our brains that may not be true and fail to serve us.

Communication tends to be more about how we say what we say than about the actual words we use. Being a clean communicator is critical to inspiring your people so they can turn on their motivational switch and Play "all iN."

A few years ago, I was at a leadership retreat. As this group of 22 people sat together, there were a few 'elephants' in the room. I didn't know what the issues were and as I listened to what was not being said, it became clear we could not move forward until we moved back and communicated about the upsets and disappointments that had caused mistrust to develop over time.

Leaders know that when they create environments where their people can come together and safely talk about the good, the bad, and the ugly, they help the team let go of the past and get engaged to move forward. You can't look forward if you are stuck in the past and when we don't get things out in the open, people hold on to what they believe is true, regardless of whether it was or will be in the future.

Leaders with courage insist people open up and have real conversations about issues and they adamantly refuse to be the go-between. They set the tone by being a clean communicator and then engage people into the real conversation.

Our co-workers are really a series of relationships and relationships are a lot like roads. Some roads are just more fun to travel on! Roads can be winding or may have pot holes. Sometimes you get off the wrong exit. The best journeys are those with smooth roads where you can see your destination. Communication paves the way to engagement, clarity of direction, and alignment.

When you open lines of communication, people will tell you a lot more than you ever imagined possible. Strive for dialogues where others are doing 60% of the talking. Be a curious listener and lead the conversation in a way that allows others to shine and align with your direction.

Having a conversation in a way that another person can hear what you have to say or "have it" as I like to say, is an art. You must balance kind with clean simultaneously. Often we think we are being nice by not saying anything which never resolves issues and tends to create more upset. Unfortunately, we get so frustrated, the communication becomes more destructive vs. constructive.

I remember a time when I worked on a team

where one person just could not get it together. They were capable of doing great work but they were always distracted due to the endless drama they attracted into their life. The only two things we could count on were their inconsistent performance and their defensiveness when others would say they had not met expectations.

It was frustrating for everyone. If it wasn't one thing, it was another and it put a lot of stress on others to pick up after their frequent messes. It took having a real conversation

> **Shiner's Tip**
>
> WHEN YOU LEAD, YOU FIND THE COURAGE TO SAY WHAT NEEDS TO BE SAID IN A WAY THAT ANOTHER PERSON CAN "HAVE IT." BEING 'NICE' TENDS TO BE MEAN. KIND COMMUNICATION IS THE SOLUTION.

(clean communication) in a way the person could hear it to help them understand that though they may not have intended to put so much pressure on others, their impact was what mattered.

"I THINK PEOPLE SHINE WHEN THEY FEEL AND KNOW WITHOUT A DOUBT THEY ARE CARED FOR. THAT SOMEONE KNOWS THEM PERSONALLY AND REALLY GETS THEM!"

Angela Haning, Director of Human Resources,
Hyatt Regency Phoenix

I move from a place of compassion when my heart sincerely cares about another.

I show compassion when I hold another person in a space of acceptance even if I am not in agreement.

I express my compassion when I feel empathy and sympathy for someone who is struggling.

I love with compassion when I let go of judgmental feelings and honor another person's reality however different from mine.

Compassion is something I give and in exchange my heart feels peace.

Compassion is like glue. It bonds us through emotion and helps us feel safe. Compassion allows us to accept another person's differences and honor their individuality.

Shiner's Tip

SHINERS KNOW THAT OTHERS CARE WHEN THEY KNOW YOU CARE! GIVE COMPASSION WITH ABUNDANCE.

It can be challenging to find compassion when others let us down or fail to meet our expectations as we can become disappointed and angry. When we choose to be supportive and yet unwilling to enable, we commit a deliberate act of compassion.

Kicking a person when they are down is a loser mentality. The Shiner's mentality is to reach out and shine the light when a person is down and work to avoid being judgmental. Sometimes refraining from judgment is the toughest part of being compassionate.

OUR CHARACTER SHINES THROUGH WHEN WE LIVE WITH COMPASSION.

"ALIGNMENT IS ABOUT EMOTION. IF YOU DON'T DEAL WITH THE EMOTIONAL ELEMENT, YOU CAN'T GET ALIGNMENT. YOU HAVE TO BRING PEOPLE TOGETHER ON SOME COMMON GROUND WHERE EVERYONE FEELS INSPIRED."

Niki Leondakis, CEO, Two Roads Hospitality

Organizations that shine have people throughout their organization — top to bottom — that lead and align with their higher purpose. Your higher purpose is your deeper reason for existing as an organization. This is at the heart of your culture.

Culture is like the heart of the body. If you have a good one, you have a healthy life and workplace. If you have a bad one, the opposite is true. All organizations have a culture; the differentiating point is its health.

Niki Leondakis, the CEO of Hotels & Resorts for Two Roads Hospitality leads visionary, high-performing teams and is known for creating award-winning workplace cultures in order to drive innovation and guest loyalty. Here, she explores what higher purpose meant when merging companies and cultures a number of years ago.

"There had just been a merger of two companies and they had very different cultures, brand styles and identities. The company had a name and the new brand was defined, but no one was working as a team. There was no shared vision so we started with stepping back and asking our leaders to think about why they got into the hospitality business.

This discussion led us to some common ground which created a starting point for a conversation on why we are here as an organization. I asked this team to envision the future — a company that was everything you wanted it to be. Everyone worked to define what the higher purpose would be and this allowed people to shed the past and look into the future.

After we defined our higher purpose, I made it clear that you are now either "on the bus" or off it. You are to be an advocate for this culture. You are not a passive bystander.

Together, we created the Spirit of Commune. It became our heart."

Leaders who want Shiners on their team help team members emotionally connect their work and its importance to the organization's higher purpose. It does not matter the position, the tasks, or the responsibility. What matters most is how each person's work is relevant to living "our why" and acting in alignment with our values: "how we do things around here."

If your people are doing the work just for a paycheck, they will do it differently than if they do it because they are inspired by how their contributions matter. What the company stands for inspires engagement.

As a leader, you have to understand how your work and the work of your team contributes to the vision of the company. Inspiring leaders who help people connect the dots between what they do and "the why" help them turn on their motivational switch, regardless of their work product. It is just that simple.

Pillar 5: Participation - Engagement

"PEOPLE LIGHT UP WHEN THEY ARE RECOGNIZED. RECOGNITION CREATES ENGAGEMENT AND THE MORE ENGAGED PEOPLE ARE, THE MORE ENTHUSIASTICALLY THEY CONTRIBUTE."

Greg Miller, VP Operations, Two Roads Hospitality

What is so appealing about video games? What makes people sit and play them for hours on end without even noticing the passage of time? Ask any game designer and they will tell you it's because the best games engage the players. The environment itself is engaging, creating a world that appeals to the senses.

How we play reflects how we live. People who are indifferent experience their work and life at a lower energy level than those who play full out.

Engagement on your team is simple: you have to make it meaningful so people play "all in."

> *Shiner's Tip*
>
> EVERYONE WANTS TO BE RECOGNIZED FOR THEIR TALENT OR CONTRIBUTION

If you want people to play "all in," you have to play all in. You also have to create an inspiring environment that recognizes those who do. We naturally engage when we feel connected and important. Clearly, a person who feels valued is more likely to engage than the reverse.

At the heart of engagement is a sense of competency and the knowledge that our contributions matter. For most achievers there is no worse feeling than that of feeling incompetent. For the highly tenacious, incompetence can be a motivator but for many, it slows our willingness to learn and grow. Under any circumstance, the feeling of incompetence feels crappy and makes it harder to contribute. This becomes an internal disconnect which limits a person's ability to shine.

> **Shiner's Tip**
>
> HOW PEOPLE ENGAGE IS
> a REFLECTION OF THEIR
> ENVIRONMENT.

Leaders who help their people become extraordinarily competent create a sense of pride as pride is a derivative of competency. This is how a culture that values learning and risk-taking raises the bar, making an environment where individuals want to actively participate so they can shine.

Organizations where people are afraid to make mistakes may appear to make fewer mistakes but what they truly lose is their ability to evolve. Nothing new happens with the same old way of thinking and doing. Encouraging your people to learn, grow, and make mistakes gives them a feeling of safety, allowing them to willingly stretch.

> **Shiner's Tip**
>
> PLAYING all iN IS aN EMOTIONAL
> COMMITMENT THAT CaN BE
> INSPIRED BUT NOT DEMANDED.
> AS a LEADER, HOW PEOPLE
> PARTICIPATE REFLECTS YOU.

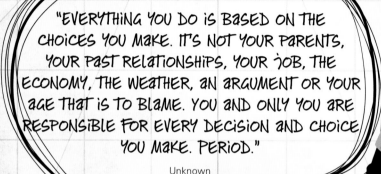

"EVERYTHING YOU DO iS BASED ON THE CHOICES YOU MaKE. iT'S NOT YOUR PaRENTS, YOUR PaST RELaTiONSHiPS, YOUR JOB, THE ECONOMY, THE WEaTHER, aN aRGUMENT OR YOUR aGE THaT iS TO BLaME. YOU aND ONLY YOU aRE RESPONSiBLE FOR EVERY DECiSiON aND CHOiCE YOU MaKE. PERiOD."

Unknown

When it comes to your life, there is only one person responsible for it…You! No one else. If you don't like your life, change it. If you feel that you aren't living your dreams, decide what you will do differently to have what you want. If you don't have time for you, make time.

Shiner's Tip

IT'S YOUR LIFE. OWN IT.

Choosing to blame and shame others limits your potential, sucks your energy, and limits your shine! When you do not take responsibility, you become a victim. When you take on more responsibility than you should by enabling others or stepping in and not allowing them to take responsibility for themselves, you become a martyr. Make the choice to design the life you want.

The goal is to be 100% responsible… no more and no less.

This is true in your personal life as well as your work world. Responsibility holds you accountable for your actions, impact and perspective. Without it, you fail to meet obligations and tend to blame others when things go wrong. Blaming and shaming is an unhealthy perspective. Shiners own their shit and make things happen so they have the life they want.

Shiner's Tip

THE 6 PILLARS ARE CENTRAL TO BEING A SHINER. BE INTENTIONAL AND LIVE THEM EVERY DAY!

TAKE NOTE & CAST YOUR LIGHT

chapter 7

The Power of Pride

"WHEN WE SHINE, OTHERS NOT ONLY NOTICE, THEY WANT TO BE NEAR US. THEY ARE INSPIRED BY US."

Renie

Pride is like electricity. Like a light switch, when you turn it on, it energizes people. Your job is to turn it on through engaging, inspiring and aligning your team members. Now you have illumination!

When people feel pride, they synergize. They do the right things without being asked. They make things happen for they feel confident and know the accomplishment will feel good. It just feels right.

WHERE DOES PRIDE COME FROM?

In a word, confidence. Confidence is healthy, as it comes from self-worth or self-esteem, and healthy self-worth makes for a dynamic and engaged human. Sometimes a person may appear to have a high sense of self-worth when in actuality, they don't. This tends to present itself (and be perceived) as egotistical.

Egotistical is defined as "excessively conceited or absorbed in oneself." It tends to come forward when we are not confident as opposed to when we are. Ego can be dangerous as it puts your "self" on the line... when you focus on your importance and what you do vs. your behavior as it relates to who you are. It's human doing vs. human being.

Pride is reflected in two primary forms:

1. CONFIDENCE: HEALTHY

2. EGOSTISTICAL: UNHEALTHY FOOLISH PRIDE

When we are moving from a place of ego, everything we do or have defines who we are vs. defining ourselves through how we live and act. It is a heavy burden to take each activity and have it define you. The pressure sets you up to only have foolish pride.

When ego is our driver, our self is on the line. This pressure leads us to shirk responsibility for our mistakes when things go wrong. We see mistakes as weaknesses so we blame others. In an egotistical state of mind, we act prideful but worry that if we let down our guard, someone will find out we are imperfect and how we want to be perceived. We all know these people and though we may not like it, sometimes we may see that same lack of responsibility in ourselves. Owning "our stuff" is what a confident person does. Blaming or shaming others is when our ego is at work.

Do you remember John McEnroe, the tennis pro? Rarely did he take responsibility for a bad shot. It was always the lineman or the referee's fault! On occasion, that may have been true. Nonetheless, he wasted tons of energy creating head trash for himself which sometimes positioned him to lose the match.

There is no peace when your energy is driven by ego. You are only as good as your last accomplishment and over time, this pressure leads to stress that will syphon your potential.

On the other hand, confidence is healthy pride. Confidence comes from that sense of competence that makes us feel good about how and what we contribute. The coaches in our lives help us feel and become consciously competent. This is why onboarding a new employee or training someone into a new position is so important.

Sarah was a top performing sales person. She knew how to make it rain! She had strong skills, a killer mindset, and strong sales processes. Every year she kicked ass over her goals and took on more territory. Then someone decided to promote her. She became the team leader and it all went downhill from there.

Initially, Sarah was excited to be recognized for her outstanding performance with a promotion. Every day she would come in and cheer on her team. She would **tell** them everything they needed to do. She thought that if she told them, they would be successful. Unfortunately, no one likes to be told what to do… if you don't believe me, ask any four-year-old!

In time, she started to create rapport breaks with her people which spiraled downward into a lack of connection and respect. Her team did not feel inspired nor supported and were no longer self-motivated. The team's synergy was unraveling. Sarah knew something was wrong. She just didn't know what it was. She was frustrated and so were her people.

Her bosses discussed, "What happened to Sarah? She has a bad attitude. No one likes her anymore and our numbers are trending in the wrong direction. Maybe we should start our exit strategy. She's not going to make it."

What happened to Sarah? She was unconsciously incompetent in this new position and her leaders were at the heart of her failure. Sarah did not understand the responsibilities of her new position. She, along with the bosses, thought that being good at her prior position would make her good at the new one. They thought she would inherently know how to be a good leader. These responsibilities, however, were mutually exclusive. No one helped Sarah understand that knowing how to do something doesn't mean you know how to lead and coach others to achieve similar results.

Sarah learned to be a great sales person over years of practice, success and failure. She gained no coaching skills in the process of taking over the new job and then as a leader she needed to learn to help others become highly competent sales people. She needed to inspire them to turn on their motivational switch so they too could shine.

With the new promotion, Sarah's skill set as a leader didn't reside in her ability to sell. It sat with her ability to develop, lead and support others.

Sarah failed for a while. Fortunately, she had a boss that helped her understand her real job responsibility. She rebounded, quickly becoming competent and confident. She now runs a Fortune 500 sales organization.

Highly competent people make a leader's life undemanding. When your people are competent, it becomes easy for you – and your customers – to recognize them. This acknowledgment of their performance encourages even more performance... and pride turns on! As pride grows, it flips their motivational switch.

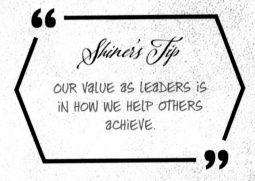

Shiner's Tip

OUR VaLUE aS LEaDERS iS iN HOW WE HELP OTHERS aCHiEVE.

Competent people participate differently from others. They are confident rather than egotistical. An egotistical performer is less likely to sustain success and rarely helps others jump on the success band wagon. They fear another person's success could decrease their worth and they question their own value. A confident performer, on the other hand, realizes "a RiSiNG TiDE LiFTS aLL BOaTS."

Bold questions for committed leaders to consider when developing competency in their people:

1. WHAT IS HOLDING PEOPLE BACK AND WHAT TRAINING MUST WE DO TO MAKE SURE THEY CAN PERFORM IF THEY CHOOSE TO?

It always stuns me when managers complete a training program and expect everyone to immediately know how to do everything shared. If you look at a child learning to ride a bike, you see that just because you show them how to ride, doesn't mean they can. And even if they get on that bike and ride it, they only get good with practice, time and desire. Desire comes from within and can be stimulated by someone enthusiastically encouraging them.

2. HOW CAN YOU CREATE ENVIRONMENTS WHERE YOUR PEOPLE WANT TO PASSIONATELY PARTICIPATE?

Participation happens when we feel like our contributions matter and they matter when we feel competent. When you don't know what you are doing, you feel fear, worry and annoyance rather than pride. You don't want to be noticed because you know you aren't shining! You feel crappy. And for most people, crappy is not a motivator.

3. **WHAT OBSTACLES DO I NEED TO REMOVE SO THE PEOPLE I WORK WITH CAN SOAR?**

When we feel pride, we are motivated to do whatever it takes. Think about it... why does one person see a piece of paper on the floor and bend over and pick it up while another person walks right on by? We don't need training on how to pick up a piece of paper! The person who exhibits pride will do things without being asked because it's the right thing to do. And the right thing comes from that sense of pride they feel.

Pride accelerates the potential of your organization. When you create alignment and add in pride and trust, you never have to worry about your financial performance again! Your people will make decisions that align with your culture and focus on your goals. They will want to shine. Now we're talking bright lights!

TAKE NOTE & CAST YOUR LIGHT

chapter 8

Everyone can Choose to Inspire

"FIRST THEY IGNORE YOU, THEN THEY LAUGH AT YOU, THEN THEY FIGHT YOU, THEN YOU WIN."

Unknown and most often attributed to Mahatma Gandhi

Check this guy out. Every few days he arrives at the beach with his umbrella in tow. He is a fan of poetry and of Robert Frost, in particular. With the end of his beach umbrella, he shares a poem in the sand.

This homeless man chooses to inspire and lead us to think. To imagine. To love poetry.

He cares about how his message is delivered, ensuring that the lettering is clear and the lines are uniform. He engages us all into reading what he has shared. He takes time to select each poem and we stand by, patiently waiting for his next inspiration. We want to know him because he touches our hearts.

This is a leader and a Shiner.

Without knowing more about him, some would ask, "Why is he wasting his life like this?" The truth is, he touches lives through his choice to engage us into his world.

Never underestimate your ability to touch another person's life.

Shiner's Tip

PEOPLE WHO SHINE,
SHINE THE LIGHT ON
OTHERS AND IN DOING
SO THE LIGHT REFLECTS
BACK ON THEM.

We can all inspire. We tap into this ability by how we look at others and at life. When we move from a space of gratitude and respect, we can find what is right in another human being and change their day in a nanosecond. The opposite is also true and that lack of light limits who we can be.

Take a look around. As bad as it might seem at times, there is always much to be grateful for... you just have to look and see. If you can't find it within yourself, honor others. Offering appreciation to another gives them a kernel of hope.

Imagine a world where each of us found one person every day and gave them an intentional and inspiring gift of acknowledgment or appreciation?

Pollyanna?
Hell, no!

When we feel inspired, we turn on our motivational switch. We engage. We want to learn and do more. We care more deeply. We impact others. We become givers. This creates an energy that connects us and this connection turns up the light. The brighter the light we create, the more we feel energized! This inspires us to do even more.

Our ability to shine has nothing to do with our title, the car we drive or someone else's definition of success. We shine by how we engage, lead and contribute – in our work and our lives.

We shine because of who we are and how we live. It is in our ability to live our life with joy.

We define our own joy and our own boundaries. We decide how we will live and how we will touch other people's lives. The light is in all of us... we just need to make sure it is fully illuminated!

WHEN WE LIVE WITH GRATITUDE, FINDING WHAT IS RIGHT IN OTHERS AND IN OUR LIVES, WE FIND HAPPINESS. AND BY GIVING THIS GIFT TO OURSELVES AND OTHERS, WE FIND MORE JOY IN OUR LIVES.

IT IS JOY THAT POWERS OUR SOULS.

Shiner's Tip

BE THE LIGHT OF YOUR LIFE.

TAKE NOTE & CAST YOUR LIGHT

chapter 9

The Allure of Negativity

"IT ISN'T ABOUT IF THE GLASS IS HALF EMPTY OR HALF FULL.
IT'S IF YOU WANT TO DRINK WHAT'S IN THE GLASS!"

Renie

We all have moments when we blame and shame others in an attempt to make ourselves feel better. This destructive pattern limits our potential and that of our team. Ineffective teams hurt everyone.

When it comes to negativity, people in this state of mind obsessively focus on what is wrong and their opinions tend to be loud and draining. Their incessant need to belittle, bully and minimize progress impacts an organization's effectiveness. Working teams with high levels of negativity inadvertently give their competitors an advantage.

There is a direct correlation between negativity and its impact on productivity over time. Teams can withstand a negative drain in short intervals but over time, the impact is substantial. Negativity decreases emotional connection between team members and causes communication to become "dirty." Environments with high productivity and low positivity (what we call Command and Control Environments), display team member burn out so eventually, even productivity declines.

In addition, 'Command and Control Environments' are highly directive and have high turnover. Though initially efficient, they cannot sustain productivity due to alignment issues and lack of trust.

Of course, the opposite is also true. Environments displaying only high positivity with low productivity tend to be more of a 'Country Club' than a high performance organization. They are friendship-based and lack focus.

They tolerate incompetence to avoid hurting anyone's feelings which results in low levels of accountability. 'Country Club Environments' are as dysfunctional as 'Command and Control Environments' because eventually, the lack of results will cause people to get fired. No productivity means no profitability. It's just math! When people lose their jobs and feel it is unfair that the rules changed (as they surely will when profitability suffers), it will trigger widespread negativity.

Negativity, though unhealthy on every level, can be a powerful, manipulative tool. It can redirect a productive conversation, making it unproductive. Negativity focuses on problems vs. solutions. It can overwhelm or make people believe there is no chance of success or happiness. With this perspective, the odds are they are right.

"IF YOU THINK YOU CAN'T SUCCEED, PLAN ON IT?"
A Strategist

Negativity triggers fear and worry and stirs up questions. Over time, negativity zaps your energy. It starts off slowly and before you know it, you are exhausted! You become indifferent and as you lose more energy, you become part of the problem. Negativity does not inspire much of anything, with the exception of more negativity. Today, negativity seems to be fueling our conversations.

Michael Bloomberg said it best:

"BEING PISSED OFF IS NOT A PLATFORM FOR CHANGE."

If negativity is so bad for our minds and souls, why is it so alluring to some people? Negativity gives people an "out." It positions people to place blame somewhere else and not take responsibility for their own actions. It can minimize another person and in some pathetic way, make us feel better about ourselves. It plays to our egos rather than our senses of confidence and compassion. Negativity takes us off the hook for owning our lives.

Negative people are petty. They speak to what is wrong with no interest in a solution. They look for perfection and minimize options, manipulating others into thinking there is no other way. This could be the negativity mantra: "What else can we do but throw our hands up in the air and give up hope?"

Negativity creates human head trash. Head trash is a leading cause of limiting your potential and ability to shine. It masks what our minds can actually imagine. Head trash focuses you on what is wrong rather than what is right. It makes it more difficult to envision what you can do to achieve what you want. It highlights the limitations and gives us a sense of scarcity vs. abundance.

I fly a lot and there are certain airports where the TSA personnel are happy and efficient. They smile, engage, say hello, do their jobs well, and are committed to our safety. You can just feel it.

In airports where the lines are long and the processes ineffective, the people seem negative and rude by contrast. I can get into line and feel the negativity swirl around me! I have to fight the urge to become a part of it. Imagine how bad it must feel for the TSA agents who work there every day!

FACT: Regardless of the airport, most of these people work for the same company: the U.S. Government. They have the same job description. The same tools. The same training, etc. What is the difference? Onsite leadership.

It is the leader's job to fanatically squash negativity. It is a cancer that eats away at progress and gains momentum through more negativity. The best tool to squash negativity is to shine the light on what is right and where you can go as an organization. To engage people into the conversation(s) of how to proceed together and become better. Leaders give us a reason to care and help us see what is possible. They change a negative or difficult situation's trajectory.

SQUASH NEGATIVITY NOW!

Leaders who inspire us help us move forward. Forward momentum creates progress and progress drives us to new solutions and better results.

High productivity environments that also have high levels of positivity are called 'A Community of Leaders.' These organizations, regardless of size, are aligned and inspired and have challenging goals. They are proactive with strong intentional leadership skills (6 Pillars) throughout the organization. They are not without challenges. It is the culture they have created and how they are led that sustains success and weathers any storm… whether economic, manpower, product or leadership-oriented.

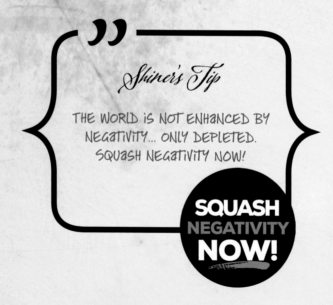

Shiner's Tip

THE WORLD IS NOT ENHANCED BY
NEGATIVITY… ONLY DEPLETED.
SQUASH NEGATIVITY NOW!

SQUASH
NEGATIVITY
NOW!

TAKE NOTE & CAST YOUR LIGHT

chapter 10

The Joy Factor

"MY MOST PROFOUND MOMENTS OF JOY HAVE ALWAYS COME FROM THE SIMPLEST OF THINGS, LIKE PEOPLE AND NATURE. THOSE ARE THINGS I NURTURE EVERY DAY TO BRING MORE JOY INTO MY LIFE. AND MORE JOY ALWAYS MAKES ME SHINE."

Jill Clark, General Manager, Mii Amo

JOY: A FEELING OF GREAT PLEASURE AND HAPPINESS

Joy is our internal shine. I first experienced this when I began playing the flute back in third grade. I will never forget the joy and pride I felt when my music teacher Ms. Yingling chose me to become a musician. I played actively for many years and was blessed with great flute teachers and conductors (leaders) who taught me a number of life lessons as playing an instrument often does.

Fast forward 30 years…
The flute recently reappeared in my world. While driving, I heard a song that contained a fantastic flute solo. I was ecstatic! I couldn't stop thinking about the jazz tune and I immediately wanted to learn how to play that song. As a classically trained flutist, I had no idea that learning to play jazz was like learning a new instrument!

Jazz flutists have only a few things in common with a classically trained flutist:

1. IT'S A FLUTE

2. THE NOTES ARE STILL THE NOTES

3. YOU NEED AIR TO MAKE THE NOTES COME TO LIFE

Outside of that, my musical world was about to have a monumental shift. Since I hadn't really played for more than 30 years beyond annual holiday songs with my sister Megan, I decided a few lessons would be in order. Megan and I made great music together over the years because she is an accomplished composer, musical producer and singer who can make anyone sound fantastic. I always appreciated this and if I was going to start playing, I would need lessons.

After I completed my first humbling lesson, my teacher informed me that though I could learn the song I had so proudly brought to him, what I really needed to learn was how to play jazz. I thought, "How hard could that be?"

Jazz is about chords. It is about connecting not just to the notes on the page, but also to the musicians sharing the stage. Jazz has soul which goes beyond rhythm. Jazz players rarely use sheet music. They memorize the tune and listen to one another to create something special, memorable and different every time. For the record, jazz is damn hard!

With classical and traditional music, you play what the composer intended. They are clear in their communication. There is a conductor or one primary leader and the solos are planned. There is no ad-libbing, no changing what is on the page, and definitely no going where no one has gone before! That is what is different about jazz in general. I had no idea that I would also be forced to change how I actually played the flute.

When you play jazz flute you change everything, from how you hold the flute to how you tongue your notes. The flute looks the same but it is really like learning a new instrument. Think of it as saying, "Well, I know English so how hard will it be to learn Mandarin?" Harder than you think!

My teacher Joseph was smart and within three weeks he had me performing on stage. He knew how to turn on my motivational switch. He pushed me and as I became more competent, I felt joy and fell back in love. And so my journey truly began.

In my crazy-busy life, I find time to practice and to go to my lessons and learn. I now play in pickup bands and open mic nights. I love playing again and I have incorporated it into my speeches to demonstrate you never know what you might find when you engage. In my case, it is more joy!

You feel joy in your life when you dare to see the world through a different view finder. When you choose not to engage, you miss out on what joy might be ahead in your world. Joy is like sunshine. It makes everything brighter.

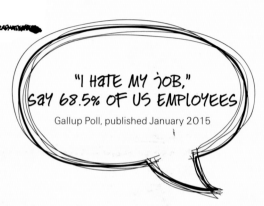

"I HATE MY JOB,"
SAY 68.5% OF US EMPLOYEES
Gallup Poll, published January 2015

That is a lot of unhappiness! When you love your work, it isn't work. It is a gift. Of course no job (or person, for that matter) is perfect. I always say, "If you love your work 80% of the time or more, you are blessed."

Feel gratitude and find joy! Where we find joy, we have happiness. And happiness makes it easy to shine.

Psychologist and TED Talk speaker Shawn Achor claims a mere 25 percent of employment success is related to I.Q. whereas factors of positivity predict the other 75 percent. Those factors including optimism, social support and viewing stress in a challenging, rather than threatening, way.

According to Achor, the brain in a positive state is 31 percent more productive than in a negative, neutral or stressed state. Achor cites a study where a positive brain greatly improved work performance. The study found sales performance increased by 37 percent and doctors' efficiency increased by 19 percent while accurate diagnosis also improved.

Joy is like anything you want. You create it! Here are a few tips to begin your joy journey:

1. ENGAGE WITH INTENTION. THE MORE ENGAGED WE ARE, THE MORE OUR CONTRIBUTIONS HELP TO CONNECT US TO OUR TEAM.
   a. Engage in your work like your life depends on it.
   b. Help others focus on what they like and love about their work. This creates joy and improves productivity in your environment as people who love their work are competent and interested in learning and growing. These are the 'fun' people. Hang with them!

2. WHENEVER POSSIBLE, DO WORK THAT LEVERAGES YOUR STRENGTHS. THE MORE YOU USE YOUR STRENGTHS, THE MORE FUN YOU HAVE. NO ONE LIKES TO FOCUS ON THEIR WEAKNESSES AND PEOPLE GENERALLY LOVE TO DO THE THINGS THEY DO WELL.

3. LOOK AT YOUR MINDSET. ASK:
   a. How is my work valuable to the organization and others?
   b. Who can I better connect with at work so I feel more a part?
   c. How does my job help me have what I want in my life?
   d. What can I do that will help me bring joy every day?

4. IF I DON'T HAVE A POSITIVE MINDSET THEN THE REAL QUESTION IS, "WHAT AND WHERE IS MY NEXT JOB SO I HAVE MORE JOY IN MY LIFE?"

5. BE REALISTIC. NOT ALL ASPECTS OF A JOB WILL BRING YOU JOY. I DON'T FIND MUCH JOY IN CONTROLLING MY FIRM'S FISCAL WASTE AND YET I HAVE TO MANAGE IT. WHAT MATTERS IS THAT YOU FIND MORE JOY THAN FRUSTRATION OR DISAPPOINTMENT.

Shiner's Tip

FINDING MORE JOY IS A DELIBERATE ACT.

When you focus on joy, you will find more happiness and trigger your motivational switch.

When I was starting out as a Regional Director of Sales, I thought my job was to have all the answers. Like most, I got the new job because I was good at the old job. In the old job I needed to have the right answers. The new job was different. I actually had to help others <u>find</u> the right answers. It was an eye-opening experience.

I remember meeting with a Managing Director. He ran the show and was not happy to have some young, immature, know-it-all come to town. Things had not been going well and I was sent in to "fix things."

I thought "fixing things" was telling people what was wrong and how to make things right. I was wrong. During that visit, I learned three things that forever changed me as a leader:

1. COLLABORATION MATTERS

2. IF YOU SEE PROBLEMS AS NAILS, YOU TEND TO USE A HAMMER. NO ONE IS FOND OF THE HAMMER.

3. GETTING THINGS DONE EFFECTIVELY THROUGH OTHERS IS THE WAY TO HAVE LONG TERM SUCCESS. DOING IT ALONE PUTS YOU ON AN ISLAND... ALONE.

I will always remember my boss's words of advice to me after that trip. He said, "Renie, when they take you to the airport it is to see your ass get on the plane."

That day I learned a lot about people and the kind of leader I wanted to become. My pursuit continues...

So what does this have to do with joy? Plenty. How we work with others brings or depletes joy. In the environment, in them, and in ourselves. When we find what is right and build on it, we inspire people to engage in solving problems openly. When we make them wrong, they become defensive. And who wouldn't be? If you want joy, create a joyful environment around you.

By the way, you can apply this to home as easily as to work.

Joy comes in many forms and from many places in our lives. When we are aware of where we have joy – and where we need more joy – we can make better decisions about our lives.

Take the chart and indicate where your joy lands using a 10 for "I don't feel much joy at all in this area" to 100, "someone scrape me off the ceiling I'm so joyful."

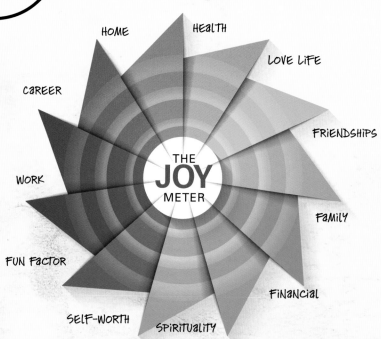

	Rating	Goal Rating	Do Differently
HEALTH	0 20 40 60 80 100		
LOVE LIFE	0 20 40 60 80 100		
FRIENDSHIPS	0 20 40 60 80 100		
FAMILY	0 20 40 60 80 100		
FINANCIAL	0 20 40 60 80 100		
SPIRITUALITY	0 20 40 60 80 100		
SELF-WORTH	0 20 40 60 80 100		
FUN FACTOR	0 20 40 60 80 100		
WORK	0 20 40 60 80 100		
CAREER	0 20 40 60 80 100		
HOME	0 20 40 60 80 100		

Joyless   Joyful

The Results:

1. WHERE YOU HAVE JOY LEVELS AT OR BELOW A RATING OF 70, YOU HAVE WORK TO DO!

2. ESTABLISH A GOAL AND THINK ABOUT WHAT NEEDS TO CHANGE FOR YOU TO FIND MORE JOY IN THIS PARTICULAR ASPECT OF YOUR LIFE.

3. PLOT YOUR PLAN AND GET MOVING!

Joy is your light. You know it when you have it! When you are down in the dumps, you not only feel a lack of joy, you tend to see things in ways that do not inspire you. Those of us with joy see things differently than those without it.

STRESS: THE JOY SUCKER

We have all heard it... Stress kills. I watched it in my father, a school teacher.

In the early years, he loved his work. He loved the kids, his sense of contribution, and the influence his coaching had on the next generation. He even loved his commute. And then things changed.

As in most education systems, budgets became extremely tight. Expectations to do more with less became increasingly unrealistic and he lost his love of the work. The stress of it all sucked the life out of him. Eventually, he could only see what was wrong with the system and he became part of the problem. He had never been a negative man... he was always so full of joy! As stress stole his joy, he no longer shined. He lived for his retirement date and died within a year of it.

You don't shine when you are overly stressed. For the most part, stress creates negativity. It does not drive innovation nor inspire people to perform at their best. Focus does. Stress puts endless limits on how we think, triggering fear and making us small. Small does not serve you or the world.

Stress doesn't really motivate you though it can make you more productive or efficient in the short term. To truly shine at our work and in our lives, we have to keep our stress levels in check. Frequently, others trigger our stress. Sometimes this is due to a lack of connection or ineffective communication. Other times it is due to unrealistic expectations, obstacles in our way, interruptions, or our own anxiety over performance.

There is nothing we can do to change other people; yet, we can manage their expectations through improving our communication and approach. To decrease stress, you must have a dialogue not a monologue. Look around! Who are you stressing out? How is that serving you or them? Look for ways to help people succeed and you will decrease their stress level and help them shine. Ask people to solve problems so they feel empowered through the process of correcting what is wrong instead of defending it.

Stress puts us in a busy-ness. Busy-ness stimulates intensity creating even more stress. Stress sucks the joy out of our lives. Remember:

- NO ONE GIVES YOU STRESS – YOU GIVE IT TO YOURSELF

- OVER-SCHEDULING ALWAYS CAUSES STRESS

- STRESS IS A VIEW OF THE WORLD THAT INCLUDES YOUR NEED TO TRY AND CONTROL IT

- CUT BACK YOUR NEVER-ENDING TO-DO LIST AND FOCUS ON WHAT MATTERS MOST

- LAUGHTER IS A GOOD CURE FOR STRESS AS IT CHANGES OUR PERSPECTIVE AND ALLOWS US TO HAVE SOME FUN

Shiner's Tip

JOY IS A KEY INDICATOR THAT REFLECTS HOW YOU ARE SHINING. THE MORE JOY, THE MORE YOU SHINE — ON THE INSIDE AND OUT.

TAKE NOTE & CAST YOUR LIGHT

chapter 11

Leveraging your Motivations

"YOUR ONLY LIMIT IS YOU."

unknown

"WHAT YOU FOCUS ON COMES TRUE."

Goals give us focus. When we are focused we are not just productive, we are also highly engaged and motivated. Motivation is a deep desire to do something… it's the reason (or reasons) a person is acting in a certain way.

When we have clarity around our motivations, we can establish goals that align with what we want in our life. When we don't know what we want, it is hard to feel motivated towards it.

I can relate. I was always highly motivated in my work with the goal to head up a sales and marketing organization. Once I achieved this goal, I wasn't sure what my next goal was! I was still energized about my work, yet I was not as motivated as I had been. I was blessed that others saw my potential and continued to promote me and it wasn't until I was offered "the next right promotion" that I realized I was aspiring to other people's dreams and not my own.

I awoke. I had lost my love for the work and knew that I had to do something different so I quit. It didn't happen because I knew what I wanted next. It happened because I knew what I *didn't* want!

It doesn't matter how you come to define your goals and dreams, it just matters that you *do!* It is through clarity that you can clearly focus and take action to support what you want out of life.

THE SHiNER'S FORMULa

A lot of research and study has been done on goal setting. Here is the approach Aspire has designed to help thousands of our clients move through a process that ensures they are focused first on the goal and their motivation toward that goal, and then the tasks they must achieve to get there. Many people start with step one and jump to step five. That only lowers your chances of achievement. This critical thinking – critical pathing process will help you think, plan and then move with focus and optimum productivity.

1. MY GOAL IS X.
Be specific. If you aren't clear, you won't focus. It has to be measurable.
Without measurement, it is just a dream.

2. DEFINE YOUR MOTIVATION...
the passion behind why you want what you want.

3. LIST THE BENEFITS
you will receive by achieving this goal.

4. WHAT IS YOUR EMOTIONAL GAIN?
How will you feel when you achieve this goal?

5. WHAT WILL YOU NEED TO DO TO GET THERE?
Step by Step.
(If you arrived at Step 5 directly from Step 1, go back to Step 2 and complete each step. No skipping!)

6. ESTABLISH YOUR STEP-BY-STEP TIMELINE,
detailed by necessary task.

7. REVIEW YOUR TIMELINE WEEKLY.
Revise and reset.

8. SETBACKS ARE JUST RESETS.
Guilt depletes us. Celebrate your reset button.

Our motivations are as individual as our finger prints. And they change with time. Leaders must be intentional in their approach to understanding what currently motivates each team member and then lead with connection and inspiration.

> **Shiner's Tip**
>
> HUMAN BEINGS ARE SELF-CENTRIC AND THE RESEARCH IS CLEAR. LEADERS NEED TO UNDERSTAND THAT THEY DON'T INHERENTLY KNOW WHAT MOTIVATES ANYONE ON THEIR TEAM. STOP ASSUMING AND START ASKING!

Recently I asked a friend what motivated her and she shared that money motivated her. I asked her what she wanted the money for and she quickly stated, "I have a horse and they are expensive. I also want to travel with my horse to shows. It all adds up."

Similar perspectives came up in my research around motivation. The fact is, money is not a motivator! Money is a vehicle to have something that is important to you. That 'something' that you want is what motivates you. You may want to make more money but the real question is: "What is it that more money will give you?" Peace of mind? Security? Funding for your child's college? Significance? Recognition?

By the way, in my research, guilt was not a motivator for anyone. Guilt is an illusion that sucks our energy and dims our light. When you miss your timeline or your goals, reset. Leave the guilt behind.

Shiner's Tip

SHINERS HAVE THE COURAGE TO PLAY BIG... TO STAND OUT AND ACTIVELY MOVE THIS WORLD FORWARD.

As a leader, you want to understand the motivation behind your goals and those of your people. When you understand what you gain by achieving each goal, you naturally turn on your motivational switch. Knowing the goal is only step one. You have to know what your real motivation is <u>behind</u> the goal.

Take fitness, for example. Many of us decide we need to get in shape around 11:45 pm December 31st of each year. We exclaim, "This is the year that I am going to the gym three times a week. I am losing weight and getting back in shape."

We may join a gym, hire a trainer, and begin our "get in shape" kick. We decide, and it is done, and yet now we have to work at it every day. We have to find our motivation behind this goal or we end up thinking about the same goal in 12 months.

Understanding your motivations and those of the people around you help you to take action and sustain it. We are all motivated for different reasons.

One thing our motivational switch research made clear was that, more often than not, people are motivated by making a difference in another person's life. What was equally interesting was that most leaders thought their team members were motivated when they felt valued, not realizing that they too wanted to make a difference in another person's life!

> "I'm motivated when I make a difference and my team is motivated when I am making them feel valued."

LEADERS AND MOTIVATION

Understanding what motivates our people is as simple as asking. I know that when I ask, I am always surprised as what I thought might motivate an individual is far from what they believe. Leaders have to align goals with the motivations of their people. If everyone is not in alignment, the team will likely be unhappy.

In researching hundreds of people, I found that many of those polled were similarly motivated and the desire to help another person and touch lives was *by far* the most common motivator.

MOTIVATOR	%
Helping Others/Touching People's Lives	33%
Pride	17%
Achieving Goals	14%
Significance/Recognition	13%
Respect	11%
Desire / Pleasure	10%
Fear / Pain	2%

Shiner's Tip

" IF YOU WANT IT, FOCUS ON IT. BE TENACIOUS ABOUT IT AND WHY YOU WANT IT. YOUR MOTIVATION DETERMINES IF IT BECOMES YOURS OR NOT. "

TAKE NOTE & CAST YOUR LIGHT

chapter 12

A Common Motivational Thread

"MY MOTIVATION COMES FROM ONE OF TWO PLACES... FEAR OR DESIRE. FEAR KICKS IN WHEN I AM ABOUT TO MISS A DEADLINE OR I AM TRYING TO MAKE A GOOD FIRST IMPRESSION. DESIRE WHEN I CAN GET A BIG CHECK AND BUY A NEW CAR OR TAKE MY FAMILY ON A FANCY VACATION."

Nic Jones, VP of Business Development, SkyTouch Technologies

We are all motivated differently and our motivations fall into one of two overriding focus areas. Fear – the absolute pain, or desire – the absolute pleasure.

PaiN | FEaR

For most of us, pain is an overriding motivator. Pain comes in varying levels and is our fears in disguise. Though fear may be an illusion, it feels real and it helps us get clarity around what we want to do differently to avoid it.

When my father was 50 years old, he had a heart attack. With the exception of smoking cigarettes, he was in good health. Smoking was a topic that had come up more than a few times in our household as his father died of lung cancer and my mother feared the same for him. She begged him for years to stop smoking.

Then one day, he stopped. According to the story he told after his heart attack and hospital stay, he was motivated by pain and fear. "Your brother was driving me to the hospital and as I sat in the back seat knowing I was having a heart attack, I realized that if I didn't make it, I would not have told my wife and children what they have meant to me. Their value in my life. The joy they have brought."

He continued, "The reality that death was a real possibility led me to promise myself that if I did make it, I would treasure life and those I loved most for as long as I had. I would tell all of you what you mean to me."

The only thing that stopped my father from smoking was the fear of dying.

EVIDENTLY HE HAD ANOTHER FEAR. WHEN THEY WERE WHEELING HIM IN ON THE GURNEY, HE ASKED MY BROTHER TO GO INTO HIS DESK DRAWER AND GET RID OF THE CIGARETTES. HE WAS AFRAID THAT IF MY MOTHER FOUND THEM, SHE WOULD KILL HIM!

Fear motivated me when I started my business 10 years after I really wanted to become an entrepreneur. Ten years earlier wouldn't have been the right time as I had important lessons to learn... luckily on someone else's dime!

I started Aspire because I had lost my passion for my work. I knew that life was too short and the worst that could happen was that if I failed, I would have to go out and find "a real job." For me, when my passion is not evident, I need to get present.

Even when I did start Aspire, many around me asked me "what will you do if you fail?" I have to say I found their perspective more annoying than scary! I had to keep those people at arm's length as their negative energy would only slow up my choice to move forward.

Fear helped me. It made me get clarity around what work I would do and what kind of company I would want to work for now that I was responsible for its destiny. I had to pay my own bills so the fear of failing was real. I grew up as a working class kid where my parents worried about the bills with every paycheck. I had no illusions of what life without a paycheck every other Friday would be like. I can remember when my father went on strike with the other teachers… the embarrassment of having to watch my mother use food stamps so we could eat during that time. The private, endless worry that we really couldn't afford my flute lessons or the other gifts my parents found a way to give my sister, my brother and myself.

My friend Brenda was my rock. She was like a sister and she believed in me. She owned her own ad agency and she told me, "If you don't want to do it alone, I'll do it with you!"

My boss Zack gave me the same vote of confidence, saying, "I want to invest in your new company."

And then my father, who had always been a raving fan, said, "I wish I had some money because I would invest in your company!"

It takes courage to dare to do something different. Fear is only challenged and overcome by the confidence in one's self and the encouragement and support of others.

"FOR ME, DESIRE IS THE KEY TO MOTIVATION, BUT IT'S THE DETERMINATION AND COMMITMENT TO UNRELENTING PURSUIT OF YOUR GOAL – A COMMITMENT TO EXCELLENCE – THAT WILL ENABLE YOU TO ATTAIN THE SUCCESS YOU SEEK."

Mario Andretti

DESIRE | PLEASURE

Desire is another key motivator as we use it to go after the things we want. The desire for money is actually the desire for what money allows us to have. The desire for love is the desire to share a safe and intimate place with another being.

Whereas fear focuses us on what we don't want, our desires ignite our dreams. They help us focus on what we want in our lives. We can have a desire for a healthy life and our commitment to that desire determines if we are disciplined enough to have it.

Our desires require different effort than leveraging our fears. With desire, we commit to put in the effort to go after what we want. We must be focused, dedicated and disciplined.

Our fears can make us change in a moment as we run from them. Our desires help us evolve over time as we move toward them. Regardless of what motivates you most, the important thing is to understand that underneath all of our motivations lie the two most powerful ones defining our actions: Fear and Pain or Desire and Pleasure.

> ## Shiner's Tip
>
> IT DOESN'T MATTER WHAT MOTIVATES YOU. WHAT MATTERS IS KNOWING HOW TO TURN ON YOUR MOTIVATIONAL SWITCH. THIS IS THE ONLY WAY TO HAVE WHAT YOU WANT IN YOUR LIFE. AND WHEN YOU HAVE WHAT YOU WANT, YOU SHINE.

TAKE NOTE & CAST YOUR LIGHT

chapter 13

Jazz Banding. Leaders Who Shine.

"JAZZ IS A CONVERSATION. EVERYONE IS WELCOME TO PARTICIPATE AS LONG AS THEY KNOW THE LANGUAGE. TOGETHER THE AUDIENCE AND MUSICIANS TELL A STORY."

Joseph Leyva, Musician (Renie's Flute Teacher!)

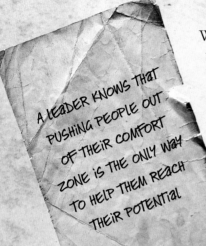

A leader knows that pushing people out of their comfort zone is the only way to help them reach their potential

We all remember that leader or coach that helped us shine. They saw our potential and pushed us towards it. Even as we may have disliked it at the time, it was a gift that made a difference in our lives.

If you are lucky enough to have leaders in your life who care about you and your growth, you know they are intentional in their approach. Their mindset is one of inspiration, discipline and engagement. They set an environment that pushes you to think and play differently.

A leader knows that pushing people out of their comfort zone is the only way to help them reach their potential and truly shine. They know that progress does not happen inside the status quo... for individuals or teams. A leader must build a platform that engages people so they find the courage to venture out and stretch. The design of this unique platform is called Jazz Banding.

Whether you are a fan of jazz or not, Jazz Banding is what happens when talented people align together and create an ever-evolving path of "sound" (or *results* in the case of most teams). The same holds true in an orchestra, a great sales team, or a sports team.

Jazz Banding is a living analogy that helps teams explore the emotions that erupt when people learn to align together through listening, exploring, connecting, and engaging from the soul. Jazz is soul music and Jazz Banding triggers the emotions needed to make people and their "music" come to life. Each of us has an instrument to play in the "band" and like jazz, there is opportunity for each person to stand out, lead, and shine. When it comes to jazz, everyone has an equally important part to play. The same is true for your team.

As you know, I am new to playing jazz though I have loved it all my life. Even after endless hours of listening, I never understood the connection between the jazz performers as they picked up their instruments and made chords come alive, creating music together. Jazz comes in many genres and all have a distinct rhythm that establishes a heartbeat for each song. Songs are stories that everyone gets to tell and in the end, the journey for the audience is ever changing. Imagine if every day your team members were disciplined enough to be that agile as they served others and delivered on your brand promise!

Like any profession, there are coaches, managers and leaders. The performers have to align, practice their craft, take lessons, improve, own their responsibility to the band, and listen to one another. To me, listening is where the magic of jazz truly lives as the music goes where the band decides at that moment. Everyone has a chance to "riff", solo and lead while the others step back and follow. This includes the person in the technical position of band leader. The leader changes based on the soloist performing and this requires everyone to stay present so they can follow and perform. It is extraordinary.

When you are Jazz Banding, you respect your team members enough to go without hesitation in someone else's direction and stay aligned. You listen carefully so you can anticipate where the journey may explore next. You move beyond your own performance to complement and support the nuances, changes and rhythms of the rest of your band. Your agility impacts the entire performance, making it better.

Shiner's Tip

LEADERSHIP NEEDS
TO PERFORM LIKE THE
MEMBERS OF a
jazz BaND.

As you move through the music (the plan), new elements will evolve and give way to new opportunities. Confidence builds and you draw in the audience (customers) so they feel the alignment of the performers and their music. Then they too come along and enjoy the journey. Without the audience, the journey is not nearly as magical.

I remember working with a large team that was integrating their international and domestic divisions into one global organization. You can imagine the turf wars that occurred... there were communication gaps in terms of language and location and many feared they would lose their jobs.

We took the team of more than 75 people "into the woods" to find common ground. We realized this was no easy task. How would we get them to begin playing together? What could they stand for? Can we get them aligned? We had one day to start the implementation of the 6 Pillars and get people to consider what might be possible if they chose to play all iN.

After a few hours of hard conversations and connection to their higher purpose, the time was right to see if they could begin to make music. Literally! Imagine 75 people all banging bongos and the horrible sound of everyone hitting them and doing their own thing. There was no beat. Too many people were trying to take charge and everyone was indifferent to the noise. As time went by, they started to realize they sounded terrible. Then one person, a true leader, stood up and set the beat. Slowly everyone started to listen and take notice. They longed for that leadership.

They wanted to make something that sounded great together instead of just making noise.

Then the magic happened. Someone else got up and added another element to the beat. Others followed. Those who had no rhythm found their place to participate through standing and dancing and before you knew it there was a Conga line.

In the beginning, no one knew what was happening or what to do. It was just a few leaders who courageously dared to set the beat. These are true leaders who engage quickly and tend to be curious and confident. The early adapters. The drivers.

Then there were those who refused to engage beyond noise and banging. Their minds set the stage for them as they sat thinking, "this is stupid. I hate this team-building crap!" These Naysayers are always slow to engage and prefer things stay as they are so they can continue their endless stream of conscious misery. Naysayers find it hard to move outside of their comfort zone and therefore never rise to their potential.

And there were those who just needed a little time to settle into the rhythm and initial chaos. They wanted a little more information and needed to start off slowly. This group tends to be the majority and as the early adapters shined the light, this group saw what was possible and began to play.

In the end, the experience was a choice. If you chose to engage, you had a different experience than if you chose not to.

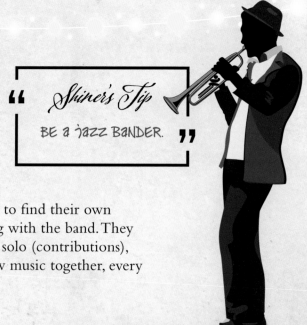

" *Shiner's Tip*

BE a jazz BANDER. "

Jazz Banding is getting everyone to find their own reason (motivation) to play along with the band. They find their rhythm, perform their solo (contributions), and enjoy as the band makes new music together, every night. Music lights us up!

TAKE NOTE & CAST YOUR LIGHT

chapter 14

What's Love got to do with It? Evidently Everything!

"LEAD FROM LOVE."

Ken Niumatalolo, Navy Head Football Coach

Leading with heart doesn't mean you don't bring your head into the game. It means you engage people through their heart. Things that touch us emotionally always inspire us to connect and connected we are stronger.

If you ask Coach Niumatalolo what his job is, he will tell you, "my real job has nothing to do with football and everything to do with inspiring men." This is the mindset of the United States Naval Academy's all-time winningest coach - the only coach with an 8-1 career winning record against Army (a major accomplishment that even a girl who doesn't watch much football must recognize!).

Then you can add the conference titles, trophies, and bowl games (to name a few of his long list of accomplishments) and you have to ask, "How does he do it?"

When I spoke with Coach, I was inspired when he responded to my question, "What is foundational in your leadership approach?"

Without missing a beat, his response was, "I lead from love."

Coaches lead us through more than the knowledge they impart on us and the skills they help us develop. They help us establish a mindset through the environments they create. The love they naturally share with us makes us want to perform better for them. When people touch our heart, something truly magical happens.

Over the years, I have seen so many people strive to keep their emotional connection flat. Flat lining is death. People don't engage without emotion and a sense of personal connection to the cause. People say "work isn't personal" and that is a lie. Our work is personal and when we feel personally responsible, we work at a far higher level than any arbitrary goal someone else set for us.

> **Shiner's Tip**
>
> EMOTIONAL CONNECTION IS AT THE HEART OF THE HUMAN SPIRIT AND WITHOUT IT, YOU CAN'T CREATE A HIGH PERFORMANCE TEAM.

Let me set the record straight. I am not an Olympian! And yet, watching the Olympics makes me proud of the accomplishments of others. It inspires me to strive for my personal best at the things I do. Watching Simone Biles was truly extraordinary and it wasn't just because of her exceptional athletic ability. It was her self-leadership. That is actually her greatest gift.

Simone goes out there and shines. She shines through her smile, her focus, her talent and her heartfelt way of supporting her teammates even when she is competing with them for the gold. Her presence made me sit up and self-examine.

In interview after interview, her inspiration came from love. Her love for her teammates and coaches. And yet, her coaches set the example of focus and discipline. They were notorious for their toughness... it was how they showed their love. Attention, for some, is love.

YOU CAN'T FAKE IT

I was recently asked, "What do you do when your boss isn't inspiring you? When you don't feel the love?"

I responded, "You have to find it from within because if you don't, you won't be the outstanding performer you were meant to be."

Know that your inspiration does not just affect you. It inspires the people around you! Learning how to lead from within means you are not dependent on others to inspire you. You have to find it within and share it with others. This is how everyone can lead.

As I travel and work with organizations, many people ask me, "How do I find energy and motivation within when others are sucking me dry?"

Here are a few tips to keep your motivational well full:

- Put space between yourself and an energy sucker. Know that their "stuff" is not your stuff.

- Read a book. Learning something new always inspires us.

- Watch a video of someone you respect on YouTube. Actually watch anything!

- Ask someone you respect to lunch. Even better, ask someone who inspires you!

- Go on a hike or a bike ride or work out and feel the adrenaline kick in

- Ask yourself, "What do I want others to say about me when they hear my name?"

- Do something you don't do well. Humility makes us more compassionate.

- Cook dinner with the people you love and just listen to their world.

- Go to a movie and laugh your ass off. Check out James Corden's "Carpool Karaoke." It is clever off the charts! Or visit aspiremarketing.com/aspire/movies for our list of movies that make you laugh, cry and pee your pants!

- Find a great coach or mentor.

- Be a great coach or mentor.

- *Mens sana in corpore sano* is a Latin phrase usually translated as "a sound mind in a sound body." Strive for both.

- Decide what your boundaries need to be so the energy suckers don't have a hall pass.

LOVE AND THE LEADER

As a leader, it is your responsibility to inspire and develop others. Your position doesn't matter. If you want to lead, you have to choose to inspire. It isn't one person's job. It is everyone's.

When it comes to leading, be authentic. People know when you are not being your true self. They sense it and it feels "icky." No one feels connected to a person who isn't authentic. It stirs up a lack of trust and trust is at the heart of playing "all in."

"CHOOSE TO GIVE LOVE. YOU WERE GIVEN AN ABUNDANCE OF IT. YOU WILL NEVER RUN OUT OF IT AND ONLY YOU GET TO CHOOSE WHO RECEIVES IT."

RC :)

People want to feel inspired and that is only experienced through an authentic heart. When we watched Ryan Lochte, the Olympic swimmer, decide to tell the truth after that night he so horribly messed up, we were still disappointed and we also felt like maybe we could trust him again.

Even at our worst, people want to believe in us... and first, they have to trust us. Our intuition takes our experience, our knowledge and our gut and tells us what to believe. And it starts with being real.

"BE REAL. PEOPLE HAVE TO BE ABLE TO RELATE TO YOU AND YOU HAVE TO BE ABLE TO RELATE TO THEM. YOU HAVE TO BE WHO YOU ARE AND THAT MEANS YOU HAVE TO SHOW THEM THE TRUTH ABOUT YOURSELF. PEOPLE HAVE TO FEEL YOUR AUTHENTICITY."

Ron Pohl, SVP and COO,
Best Western Hotels & Resorts

Shiner's Tip

THE WAY TO GET PEOPLE TO THEIR FULL POTENTIAL IS TO TOUCH THEIR HEART

Your leadership is reflected in the eyes and performance of your team. People's eyes shine when they connect emotionally. It is how we connect with others quickly and deeply that inspires them to become their best selves. Your team's light always reflects on you.

"MY JOB IS TO FIND OPPORTUNITIES AND SHINE A LIGHT ON THE YELLOW BRICK ROAD AND ENGAGE PEOPLE IN A WAY THAT COMPELS THEM TO COME ALONG FOR THE JOURNEY. THEY GET TO EXPLORE AND CONTRIBUTE AND SEE HOW THEIR PART FITS INTO THE OVERALL PLAN. FOR ME, THIS IS THE EXTRAORDINARY GIFT OF MY WORK."

Julius Robinson, Vice President,
Autograph Collection,
Marriott Hotels & Resorts

When we care enough to touch another person's heart, we also touch our own. Human emotion does not stop as we enter our workplace... It needs to strengthen there as we spend more time at work than anywhere else. The true reflection of who we are as a human being is how we make another person feel.

In life, it is not what you *do* that defines you, it is how you do it — how others feel in your presence. Your actions towards others either shine the light or dim it. You can have high expectations of those you work beside and still care deeply for them. These two behaviors are not mutually exclusive. When *you* care, *they* will care.

I'm sure you know that person who is the "office rule keeper." It's a thankless job and an important one as operational processes and procedures ensure accountability, responsibility and profitability. There are two ways for a person in this role to lead — with toughness or with firmness.

Toughness is harsh. It is extremely direct and breaks rapport. It leaves a taste of "meanness" in its wake. In contrast, firmness sets expectations in a way that makes the other person want to do it right. They may not like it and they will respect it.

When a leader uses firmness as a coaching tool, people are less defensive and more apologetic. Setting expectations is a must and sharing and managing them in a way that others feel emotionally responsible is at the core of being a heartfelt leader.

Most people are inspired by firmness and rarely excel with toughness.

SYNERGY:
the increased effectiveness that results when two or more people or businesses work together.

All organizations need guidelines and expectations to gain alignment, minimize chaos, provide constant improvement, and ensure sustainability. The leader managing the rules, regardless of title or position, has to have heart in their approach as it has a dramatic effect on how people work together, creating synergy. How you make people feel either moves them to align with you or alienates them.

Shiner's Tip

EVERYONE IMPACTS YOUR TEAM'S SYNERGY, NOT JUST THE BOSS

Where there is synergy amongst a team, there is compassion for one another. Compassion is one of the most under-respected pillars of leadership. Some see compassion as weakness, thinking it minimizes their ability to hold people accountable or communicate the truth out of fear that they will hurt the person's feelings.

As leaders, when we move from compassion we can correct a situation without disempowering a person. When a person feels empowered and honored, even when they have made a mistake, they are more likely to own the mistake and take action to correct it. The person who instead lives in a defensive state of mind moves into a "blame and shame" mindset.

Compassionate organizations gain a competitive advantage (to every team member's benefit) because when things "hit the fan" as they always do, organizations with deep levels of compassion rally together to help clean up the mess, even if they didn't make it. Commitment, like compassion, is a heart thing.

TAKE NOTE & CAST YOUR LIGHT

chapter 15

Selecting a Shiner

"HIRING IS LIKE SHOPPING... IF THE SHIRT DOESN'T FIT, YOU WOULDN'T BUY IT. AND IF YOU DID BUY IT, YOU'D DEFINITELY RETURN IT! IF THE EMPLOYEE DOESN'T FIT, YOU SHOULD DO THE SAME."

Renie

Not everyone is a good fit for your organization. A super star in one company may be a flop in another. The same holds true within the same organization. A person who is outstanding in one position can fail when promoted or transferred to another.

People far smarter than I have studied how to hire talent so I will skip the mechanics. Here is what tends to be missed in the process of hiring a Shiner:

STEP 1: TRAIN YOUR PEOPLE TO HIRE SHINERS!
As leaders we have to ensure we hire the right people. Interviewing is the single most important component of creating a team of shiners. In my research, the average manager has less than 41 minutes of actual hiring training. That's not a lot of time considering it is the single most important job a leader will do to build their team.

STEP 2: CLEARLY MAP OUT THE NON-NEGOTIABLES
There are usually four or five non-negotiables. Non-negotiables are the musts for everyone in your organization. This helps you short-list candidates, minimizing time wasted vetting the masses.

STEP 3: CLEARLY DEFINE WHAT A SHINER LOOKS LIKE FOR EACH POSITION ON YOUR TEAM
Build a checklist of traits, behaviors, attitudes and skills by position (20 to 25). Get everyone involved in building this list — especially the people who are doing the job today. During the interview process, score each person against each item on the checklist. Math has a way of helping you focus on logic rather than emotion.

STEP 4: LET'S DO DINNER

When it comes to hiring anyone in a position of leadership do the "let's do dinner" test. As people relax, you get to know them and you can decide if this is someone you would want to have dinner with again sometime soon.

CASE IN POINT

At Aspire we have everyone involved in the onboarding and development process of a new hire. We all interview, vet and vote on whether this candidate is:

1. Aligned with our culture
2. Able to demonstrate the skill set needed for competence in the position
3. A learner with agility
4. Intelligent
5. Hardworking

A candidate must score 100% on the five non-negotiables listed above. If they do meet all criteria, we then ask each person if they believe this candidate is worth their time. We estimate between 100 and 400 "other people's man hours" to bring on a new hire before they are flying solo. That is a lot of cost, commitment and coaching so we only hire if we have a 100% vote. We have learned the hard way that hiring the wrong person costs more than the wasted man hours. It causes frustration, builds bad energy, and hits our bottom line.

Everyone has a vote because once we hire this candidate our mindset is that we are "all in" to help this new hire succeed. Of course we all make mistakes. Within 30 days, we know if we don't have a good fit and we terminate. We don't need more proof. The departure is usually honorable because if the person was coached effectively, they have already come to the same conclusion.

OUR RULE: We only hire people who fit the five non-negotiables. Then we use the checklist as our guiding light, ensuring we only hire people who have the potential to shine.

Shiner's Tip

" YOU CAN'T BUILD a TEAM THAT SHINES WITH THE WRONG PEOPLE. STOP WASTING YOUR TIME! "

Characteristics of a Shiner

- Highly engaged
- Positive nature. Energized.
- Shiners make more mistakes than those who play it safe as they color outside the lines, challenge the status quo and think boldly
- Learner mentality
- Focused and tenacious
- Strong self-leadership skills: 6 Pillars
  - → Ability to connect well with others
  - → Clean Communication
  - → Compassion
  - → Higher Purpose – have passion for their life
  - → Participation/Engagement
  - → Responsible/Accountable
- Are highly self-motivated and know what turns on their motivational switch
- Highly competent at the job skill and process set
- Demanding. They want coaching, development, recognition, respect and growth. Shiners can be high maintenance.

Shiner's Tip

SHINERS COLOR OUTSIDE THE LINES. AND SOMETIMES, THEY MOVE THE LINES!

TAKE NOTE & CAST YOUR LIGHT

chapter 16

Onboarding so They Shine

"THERE IS ONLY ONE CHANCE TO MAKE A FIRST IMPRESSION. DON'T BLOW IT?"

Renie

Think of the onboarding process as part two of the selection process and chapter one of your *Being a Part of Us* experience.

Why is it part of the selection process? It is stunning to me that a leader will spend hours searching for the right person, deal with endless residual effects as the position sits empty, and then drop the ball with a half-baked onboarding plan for this new, excited person. The single most important day of a team member's employment is their first day! We give parties for people when they leave. Imagine how it would feel if you gave a party for someone who just joined your team!

Competence in most positions takes between 90 and 180 days and the first week sets the tone. This onboarding time tells you everything you need to know about how to develop and inspire this employee.

Shiner's Tip

TAKE THE TIME TO PLAN AND CLEARLY MAP OUT THE FIRST 30 DAYS. BE SURE EXPECTATIONS, SIGN-OFFS AND OPPORTUNITIES YOU WANT INCLUDED ARE PART OF THE PROCESS.

DEVELOP AN INTERNAL CHECKLIST
TO ENSURE YOUR PLAN AND TEAM MEMBERS ARE ALIGNED

CREATE A BUDDY SYSTEM
SO A NEW HIRE HAS AN IMMEDIATE SENSE OF BELONGING

MAKE THE PROCESS INTERACTIVE.
ENSURE THE LEARNING ISN'T 'KNOWLEDGE DUMPING'

REPETITION IS THE MOTHER OF SKILL.
BE SURE PEOPLE HAVE THE OPPORTUNITY TO DEMONSTRATE THEIR LEARNING.

FOR THE FIRST WEEK, HAVE A DAILY NEW HIRE CHECK-IN WITH A LEADER

Zappos is a well-known online store with a reputation for selection and service. They are also known for their high performance teams. They are fanatical about their onboarding program where employees receive four weeks of training to include culture immersion. After two weeks of classroom training, they are empowered to learn by doing as they begin taking calls with assistance. They then move through a three-week incubation period.

Zappos' training focuses on:

- Culture
- Skills
- Product

> PEOPLE WANT INCLUSION. THEY WANT TO BE A PART OF SOMETHING BIGGER THAN THEMSELVES WHERE THEIR CONTRIBUTIONS ARE VALUED.
>
> RC :)

The most powerful piece of their onboarding process is their renowned 'buyout bonus.' Zappos makes new employees an offer: If they don't feel the empowered, playful Zappos culture called 'Holacracy' is for them, they can quit and receive a month's severance. Few take the company up on their offer.

Imagine the savings, not to mention the decreased brain damage, over time. Brilliant!

Shining leaders focus on developing committed, talented people. You don't have time for people who cannot deliver or who are not demonstrating their commitment. Don't be afraid to make cuts; it is the compassionate thing to do. Share your expectations and see the bar rise!

TAKE NOTE & CAST YOUR LIGHT

chapter 17

Shine through Service

"I'VE LEARNED THAT PEOPLE WILL FORGET WHAT YOU SAID,
PEOPLE WILL FORGET WHAT YOU DID, BUT PEOPLE WILL NEVER
FORGET HOW YOU MADE THEM FEEL."

Maya Angelou

IT'S THE RIGHT THING TO DO.

Most of us thrive when we serve others. We are humbled when we help someone in need. Support and acts of kindness bring us internal gratitude, filling our hearts. Imagine a world where we would all serve one another every day. Imagine the powerful, positive energy we would all create!

Our research showed 'serving others' as the highest ranked motivational switch. It came in many forms - from 'helping people achieve their dreams' to 'watching people who work for me soar.' Regardless of the words, it was clear that the feeling of giving and supporting others triggers the motivational switch for many of us. One act of kindness every day should be a lesson we all live by.

THE WOMEN OF WINGS

I founded Wings to Fly Leadership Camps to offer young women, ages 12-18, the opportunity to connect with other girls, learn leadership skills (6 Pillars of Intentional Leadership™) and gain the mentorship of many smart, strong women leaders who have walked their own humbling and demanding paths.

"I SLEPT AND DREAMED THAT LIFE IS ALL JOY. I WOKE AND SAW THAT LIFE IS ALL SERVICE. I SERVED AND SAW THAT SERVICE IS JOY."

Khalil Gibran

Education is a tremendous act of service as it frees the mind and opens the door to all you have to offer. The women who volunteer with Girls Rule Foundation and make Wings to Fly Leadership Camps possible were mentored by others and choose to pay it forward by inspiring dynamic up-and-coming leaders as they share their time, attention and experiences.

Imagine a 15-year-old girl going to camp. At this time in a young woman's life, self-doubt is the norm. It takes courage to explore her own opinions and gifts and it can be unnerving to imagine a future while questioning her own self worth. Body image issues can drain energy. It's tricky to find the balance between being bold and beautiful in her own skin while desperately wanting to be accepted, wondering, "How do I stand out while hoping to fit in?" It's a time when she is finding the confidence to understand that being out in front means you may be an easy target.

It takes enormous courage to choose to let your dreams and ambitions soar in a world that readily accepts criticism of, and jealousy toward, those who aspire.

Wings Leadership Camps were created to help these young women feel supported, loved and respected as they become tomorrow's leaders. Unfortunately, as women we must journey through judgment of our clothing, hairstyles and personal life choices. This journey calls for a dance of balance as, with tenacity and conviction, we somehow decided to keep our mother's jobs and, in many instances, also took on our father's.

The women coaches at Wings to Fly don't get paid for their extraordinary service and many take vacation time (paid or unpaid) as the real payoffs are realized in other ways. While there, Wings coaches bond for life but the real reason they go is their commitment to the next generation of amazing women.

At Wings Leadership Camp, whether you are a coach or a leader of tomorrow, you learn to listen and serve others... to have compassion for another and identify things in your own life for which you are grateful. One way to find gratitude is to help someone else and in those moments of serving, we shine. Through service, we help others tap into the gifts they may not see in themselves. When we help others, it fills us with gratitude, sourcing our joy.

As a Wings to Fly coach, you voluntarily go to a camp where you can't work, have a glass of wine, text or call anyone. For an entire week, you are committed to someone else's daughter. In doing that, you come back physically and emotionally exhausted and you sleep for an entire day, and yet you are so invigorated, you can't wait to do it again!

As coaches, a transformation takes place... we are giving our time, energy and wisdom and we gain so much more! Every year, we are reminded that shifting to serve someone else when our tank is empty can fill us.

If you would like to have a dynamic young woman attend Wings Leadership Camps and/or would like to donate to Girls Rule Foundation, please visit www.girlsrulefoundationcamp.org

THERE aRE MaNY WaYS TO SERVE – both as individuals and in an organized team environment where service to others enhances our alignment and builds our connection with one another so the impact is both internal and external.

Serving others is why so many organizations align with charities. It gives those who want to serve an opportunity to do so in an organized way.

When we serve, we raise our consciousness. This naturally triggers a stronger sense of compassion and gratitude within our own lives.

Those who serve others offer an endless light of hope to whom they are serving. These acts of kindness fill everyone's heart whether they give or receive.

Service can be the gift of your time, energy, presence or money and it does not need to be about funding or building or giving. We can serve in so many ways. To serve is to touch another person's life in some way. It can be as simple as a hello or a smile. Regardless of your position, you can make a difference with just a sincere "how are you today?" When we genuinely care, we serve.

You may never know the impact of even a small gesture.

GOING UP?

Why is it that people don't talk in elevators? There is nothing else to do! If you observe, most people aren't even looking at their phones. They are looking up at the floor number hoping the elevator won't stop and waste a moment of their time. Talk about an opportunity to engage and touch another person's life!

People always look surprised when I ask them about their day or engage them in conversation on an elevator. Many even say, "it was nice meeting you" when we depart. We both feel better for having taken a moment to spread some positive warmth.

Service means honoring with the heart. Serving without expectation. Serving to make a difference, no matter how big or small, in someone else's world. When we are heartfelt in whatever we do, we serve. And in doing so, we touch another person's heart as well as our own.

Having worked in both the tourism and senior living service industries extensively, I have witnessed amazing acts of service – from offering to help someone having trouble transitioning into a new chapter in their life to leaving a note from the tooth fairy under a child's pillow while their family was out to dinner – thoughtful moments of caring, giving and loving another.

Serving others is a perspective of caring about them even if they may not be aligned with you. Love for others helps us strengthen our love for ourselves. It is a gift that both gives and receives. Yes, love is all there really is.

If you are asking, "Is she back to talking about love in business?" The answer is a resounding, "Yes, and love in life." When we give love, we assuage another person's hurt and this is a tremendous service.

In most companies, service is at the heart of whatever product we are selling. It is how we serve our clients that reflects our relevance in the marketplace. Clients remember and value our thoughtfulness and openness as we find ways to serve.

Products are commodities that can be duplicated. Service is not. Service is one element of your business that no one else can truly replicate. It comes through your people. They tell your story.

SERVICE iS a CULTURE

Service in business is not a training program. Service isn't a strategy either, though it does drive customer loyalty and retention. Organizations either commit to service as a culture or they do not. The more fanatical a team is committed to serving, the stronger the bond they create. Not just with their customers, but also with each other.

Defining your service culture is an intentional act. It goes beyond clarifying your vision and mission. It speaks to your brand and who you are as an organization. It speaks to your reputation and relevance. You can have the best product in the marketplace and if your people are rude, or do not have the time or resources to serve thoughtFULLY, you will lose in the market share game. Your culture tells your team what you value. It clearly defines how each person on your team will behave and ensures they make appropriate choices. A healthy service culture empowers your people to self-lead and in doing so, find opportunities to serve beyond expectations. It is through their service that your brand strengthens and their senses of pride and ownership come alive.

Your service culture clarifies your brand promise and what you stand for as an organization. It should be integrated into all of your training and coaching as repetition is the mother of skill and perspective.

When you ensure a perspective that to serve others is to honor yourself and your organization, you create a culture of substance. Smart, service-driven organizations understand that to serve means customers matter first.

YOU HaVE TO SERVE YOURSELF...

As gifted as your life may be, it is only natural to find days, weeks, and sometimes longer when we feel down or disappointed. We all get overwhelmed and it never brings out our best self!

During these times, <u>we have to serve ourselves first and in doing so, we serve others around us</u>. Here's how it works:

I always like to start with asking:
- What am I grateful for in my life?
- How am I serving others in a way that matters to them?
- How can I give today?

These questions help me change my perspective so I can move my negative energy in a positive direction, allowing me to regroup, reorganize and refocus my commitment.

When you change your perspective to serve your sense of self, you focus on what is right and you give. In the end, you serve the universe at large at the same time!

BE a GIVER.

The concept of 'pay it forward' is true. When we give, the law of the universe will ensure we receive. We may not know when or how and it just happens that way.

Be specific to your commitment to serve others and notice the gifts you receive.

- Random, daily acts of kindness and acknowledgment of others
- Volunteerism
- Philanthropy
- Help clean up a mess, even if you didn't make it
- Mentoring
- Be a service culture leader
- Notice someone in your office who needs a break or a glass of water... and provide it
- Participate and support your child's school activities
- Help a teacher out by providing school supplies
- Be a coach in business or on the field
- Fundraising for a cause you believe in

> ## Shiner's Tip
>
> IT iS iN THE PRiDE OF GiViNG THAT WE RECEiVE JOY, aND JOY iS aT THE HEART OF SHiNiNG.

I ask you:
"HOW aRE YOU SERVING?"
Because when you serve, you Shine.

Share how you are serving at www.aspiremarketing.com/aspire/shinerinservice

TAKE NOTE & CAST YOUR LIGHT

chapter 18

Shifting the Focus

"WHEN WE BELIEVE, WE ACHIEVE."

Andre Fournier, Executive Vice President, Two Roads Hospitality

YOU CAN'T SHINE AND PLAY SMALL!

News Flash: You were not put on this planet to play small. You only have a 17% chance of getting here in the first place, so understand how lucky you are to be here! What will be your mark, your imprint? People remember people who choose to be bold. They remember people with the courage to lead. People who make an impact.

WHaT iS iN YOUR WaY?

The single greatest reason we don't stand out is that we are programmed from an early age to fit in. In our early years, we are actually told to play a little smaller and to not stand out so we inadvertently create belief that we should "play it safe."

What are you waiting for? Why is it that being bold is not considered a great gift? There is no doubt that being out in front makes you an easy target and who wants to be at the back of the pack? You were born to stand out!

HOW DO YOU PLaY BiG?

- Own it. Connect with what matters most in your heart. Don't question your heart or your dreams. Own them.
- Ask yourself how you can contribute to the world. Stop piling crap on all you have to offer others!
- Don't let others shut down your dreams. No one achieves their dreams without risk and those who take the risk always end up with more than those who resent never risking anything. Resentment comes from what we didn't do, not what we did! It is head trash that stops you from moving forward.
- Change your mindset… shift your focus
- Jealousy is a negative, puker mentality. When the light is shining on you, the dimmers will emerge. Surround yourself with supportive people.
- Stay humble. The bigger you are, the more humble you should be. Let the light reflect around you.
- Stay grateful. It keeps success in perspective and slows you down to enjoy the journey.

OUR STRENGTHS EMPOWER US TO SHINE

We are all given unique gifts. Strengths that allow us to make a difference if we choose to use them. When we use them, we are likely to touch another's life. We shine.

Shiners play to their strengths: the doorway to potential. People spend way too much time focusing on their weaknesses. Organizations that focus on strengths are agile and therefore can leverage opportunities. When team members spend the majority of their day utilizing their strengths, they love coming to work! Sometimes people are lucky. Their gifts unfold easily. Others have to work hard at finding what they love. Regardless, your best self lies in leveraging your strengths.

"IT IS THROUGH HONORING THE GIFTS THAT YOU HAVE BEEN GIVEN THAT YOU HONOR THE PERSON YOU WERE MEANT TO BE AND THIS ALLOWS YOU TO MAKE A DIFFERENCE EVERY DAY IN SOMEONE'S LIFE."

Theresa Dileo, Director of Human Resources, Sea Island Resort

Our mind is in the driver's seat of our life. It tells us what direction we can and cannot go. It helps us and it hurts us. Our brain only shifts when we change our focus. The key to changing focus is changing perspective.

Perspective comes from our thoughts. It is hard to let go of limiting and fearful thoughts when we risk losing what we have (even if what we have is not what we want). Perspective changes when you change the questions you ask yourself. The questions you ask yourself (self-talk) determine the trajectory of your life.

The same is true as a leader of a team. If the question you ask is, "how will we make these crazy, ever increasing goals?" you will not inspire people to think about how to achieve them. Likely, they will think about how crazy the goals are.

If you were to ask the same group different questions, inspiring them to think about the potential and possibilities, you would end with a different result. For example, "how do we evolve into our next chapter?" or, "If we could do anything to enhance our growth, what would we do?"

POWER QUESTIONS FOR LEADERS

1. What would we have to do to double our success? What would need to change about our people, our processes, our skills and our focus?
2. What will we create next? Not what can we – can isn't a mindset of a Shiner!
3. What brand touch points should we innovate?
4. What obstacles must we remove so our people can shine?
5. What is holding us back? How can we think about it differently?
6. Who can help us think differently?

POWER QUESTIONS FOR SHINERS

1. What motivates me? This is where your greatest 'self' lives and contributes.
2. How does it come through in the work I do?
3. What kind of leader do I want to be in the future?
4. How am I getting in my own way? How can I get out of my own way?
5. What are my real dreams? When you are living them you have a life of joy.

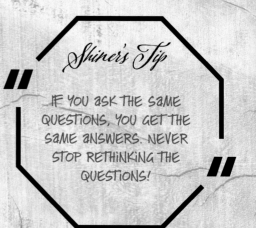

Shiner's Tip

IF YOU ASK THE SAME QUESTIONS, YOU GET THE SAME ANSWERS. NEVER STOP RETHINKING THE QUESTIONS!

TAKE NOTE & CAST YOUR LIGHT

chapter 19

The Choice is Yours

"YOUR CHOICES REFLECT YOUR LIFE. CHOOSE WISELY."

Renie

To be a Shiner is simply a choice. Why some people don't choose to truly let themselves shine often rests in their fears. Fear is an illusion. It is our little people in our brain "talking trash." Fear is the leading killer of all potential and your ability to shine. Fear can douse your light.

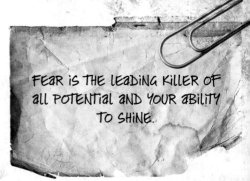

FEAR IS THE LEADING KILLER OF ALL POTENTIAL AND YOUR ABILITY TO SHINE.

Our fear of not being good enough is at the source of why we don't become all we were intended to be. The real question to ask yourself is: what do you have to lose?

The quality of your life is a reflection of your choices. You're in control of your choices and your perspective so you have all the control you actually need!

Today things are moving fast. Our never-ending To-Do List is longer than ever. We find ourselves with less time and more to do.
- What is happening?
- Why does life seem so out of control?
- Why are we less tolerant? Less thoughtful? More aggressive? Less hopeful?

We are a world in great transition. Transition is like an awakening – it is time to check in and reflect.
- Where am I in my life's journey?
- Do I find joy in my work?
- Do my relationships enhance my life or do they detract from it?
- How am I serving others? How do I contribute to the world at large?

All great questions and ones you have to answer thought-FULLY if you really want to shine. This is self-leadership: seeing each day as an opportunity to lead and to transform our lives as we want them to be.

Stop putting energy into things and people who don't give back. Put your energy to good use! Know that everything you want in your life is available to you. Believe in yourself. Don't let anyone let you think you aren't good enough.

Shiner's Tip

DON'T BE AFRAID OF CHANGE. BE AFRAID OF NOT CHANGING.

Whether you are leading a team or you are the leader inside your home, your leadership inspires people to engage. You can only give them a reason. They have to do the rest. You can inspire them and they have to turn on their motivation switch!

Ultimately when people choose to participate, they have a completely different experience. Some curious and courageous people are fast engagers so they actively participate. Others are slower as they need more certainty.

How they see you participate as a leader influences how they choose to participate. If you aren't a participator, odds are your people won't be either. Leadership is a behavior, not a position. Engagement is about inspiring people to participate. Your job is to help shine the light so they choose to engage... so they choose to be "all in."

THE CHOICE TO SHINE IS SOLELY YOURS!

TAKE NOTE & CAST YOUR LIGHT

chapter 20

The Little Guide to Shining

"ALWAYS LOOK TOWARDS THE SUN."

Kim Tesori

1. BE THE LIGHT:

Know what matters most in your life and bring it to life a little every day in some way.

2. WHY SHINE?

We not only make a difference in our own lives, we make our own mark on the world! Keep shining your light…

3. PASSION IS YOUR FUEL:

To live your life with passion is to honor yourself and awaken your potential. Shiners don't fear their passion. They embrace it and wear it with pride!

4. ENVIRONMENTAL HAZARDS:

Your environment is critical to your ability to perform and shine.

5. WHAT DOES IT MEAN TO SHINE?

Demotivating thoughts limit your potential. Motivating thoughts turn on your motivational switch.

6. LEADERS SHINE THE LIGHT:

How you lead yourself tells the story of your life. It tells who you *are*.

7. THE POWER OF PRIDE:

Developing competent people is a commitment. When someone gets a new job, the team helps them become competent, quickly creating pride and enthusiasm. With pride, people shine!

8. EVERYONE CAN CHOOSE TO INSPIRE:

Shining is not just a leadership trait. Shining is a human trait. It is a choice we make. Everyone can be a Shiner!

9. THE ALLURE OF NEGATIVITY:

The world is not enhanced by negativity… only depleted. Squash negativity NOW!

10. THE JOY FACTOR:

Finding more joy is a deliberate act.

11. LEVERAGING YOUR MOTIVATIONS:

If you want it, focus on it. Be tenacious about it and why you want it. Your motivation determines if it becomes yours or not.

12. A COMMON MOTIVATIONAL THREAD:

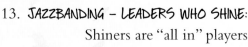

Our motivations reflect what we value and why we value it.

13. JAZZBANDING – LEADERS WHO SHINE:

Shiners are "all in" players

14. WHAT'S LOVE GOT TO DO WITH IT? EVIDENTLY EVERYTHING!

Love is at the heart of all motivation– love for one's self, love for your passions, love from a leader, love of life, love of others... love makes us shine.

15. SELECTING A SHINER:

You can't build a team that shines with the wrong people. Stop wasting your time!

16. ONBOARDING SO THEY SHINE:

Plan and clearly map out the first 30 days. Be sure the process includes outcomes, opportunities, checks and balances. Share your expectations and see the bar rise!

17. SHINING THROUGH SERVICE:

You shine when you serve others. How are you serving others? How are you giving?

18. SHIFTING THE FOCUS:

You are responsible for developing your skills so you can shine. Stop waiting for others to do it for you. Do it for yourself. You deserve to be recognized as a shiner!

19. THE CHOICE IS YOURS:

Shining is a choice you make. It's deliberate and demanding.

This list was designed to give you quick reference and reminders from key points in each chapter of *aspire... to shine.* It is an excerpt from my MiniBük *The Little Guide to Shining©* which contains an inspirational and educational list of Shiner Tips. If you would like a copy (while supplies last), email: **info@aspiremarketing.com**
or visit: **www.aspiremarketing.com**
and complete the request form online.

#BeAShiner

All in,

Renie

"SHINE THE LIGHT."

Remie

ACKNOWLEDGMENTS

To my mother, Barb who has spent a lifetime shining the light so women like myself can live to their full potential.

To my father, Tommy, who told me that my passion would be my gift and to always bring my good time with me.

To my sister Megan and brother Seth who never stop believing in me and to my brother Tommy who taught me to embrace life.

Enid Vein, you were the best coach a person could ever have had. You made me shine. I miss you!

To my sisters: Nancy, Rita, Wizzy, and the list goes on... Through thick and thin... #gratitude

To Brenda who encouraged me to start Aspire 22 years ago with these exact words, *"Renie, you've got this!"*

To JC, Barbara, Misha, Kim, Marisa, Amy, Kendall, Liz, Debbie, and all of the leaders of Aspire around the globe. Each of you has inspired me and in doing so, you have touched my life immensely.

To Jeffri-Lynn for being my amazing editor and for always respecting 'my voice.' Not to mention putting up with my crazy-ass Self!

And lastly, to Dolf for giving me Bella and to Bella, who shines brightly every day. You are joy.

All in,

Renie

AUTHOR

Renie Cavallari is an award-winning strategist known for innovation, creativity, and cutting-edge change navigation which she employs to ensure client relevance now and into the future.

As founder, CEO, and Chief Instigator of Aspire, a company whose client retention rate hovers above 96% year-over-year for 22 years, Cavallari uses extensive, field-tested research as the basis for revolutionary training programs that engage, entertain, and inform even as they improve financial performance and drive measurable results for companies all over the world.

An internationally recognized leadership expert, This CEO Coach is a captivating speaker and the author of six other works, including the first two in the *aspire to...* series:

The Official Girlfriends' Getaway Book
Aspire... to Be (the first in the Aspire... to series)
Aspire... to Lead (the second in the Aspire... to series)
Live. Love. Laugh. Often... A book of poetry
**Business is Like Baseball*
**The Little Guide to Shining*

*available on Amazon and via aspiremarketing.com
**available via aspiremarketing.com
or email: info@aspiremarketing.com